Transformative Parenting™

Transformative Parenting™

The Empathic, Empowering Approach to Optimal Parenting and Personal Growth

Edward V. Haas, MD

Full Life Press
New Jersey

Publisher:

Full Life Press, LLC
Jersey City, New Jersey U.S.A
Contact: info@fulllifepress.com

Disclaimer:

The information and advice given herein should be considered carefully in light of the reader's unique life circumstance. The author and publisher disclaim all liability for direct or consequential damages resulting from relying on the material contained in this book.

Parents should discuss childcare and child development concerns with their pediatrician or family doctor. Reading this book does not establish a doctor-patient relationship between the reader and Dr. Haas.

ISBN: 978-0-9963408-5-4

Library of Congress Control Number: 2015908485

Dedication

To the memory of Barbara Ceglowski.

Acknowledgements

Unfortunately, it is not possible to thank everyone who helped to make this book possible. Family, friends, teachers; even strangers, whose chance encounters have left lasting impressions over the years - and authors, whose names are largely forgotten, but whose ideas were not.

I thank Kim Haas, Rosa Lewis, Loretta Haas, and Sylvia Perera for reading and commenting on an early draft of this book. Kim challenged me to do a better job of explaining my ideas. Rosa encouraged me to offer more examples. Loretta's meticulous editing and insightful comments regarding style were extremely helpful. I thank Sylvia for her wisdom, knowledge and steady support.

We must all acknowledge the profound influence of childhood, and particularly our parents, in shaping who we are. My mother's example instilled the capacity for selfless love, and single-minded devotion, while my father taught me self-reliance, and the belief that if anyone can do it, I can do it; traits instrumental to the development of Transformative Parenting, and the writing and publishing of this book.

Finally, this book would not exist if it were not for my wife Kim, and my daughter Gabriella, who each in her own way provided the motivation to make it happen.

Preface

Feeling strongly that you have been given an important message to share with the world is a decidedly mixed blessing.

On the one hand, there is a sense of purpose, a reason to get up in the morning, which gives meaning to your life and lends preciousness to every moment.

I have come to believe that my life has been carefully designed to teach me, and motivate me to teach others, about what I am calling Transformative Parenting™.

On the other hand, I struggle with anxieties and forebodings: Will people listen? Can they be motivated to change? Am I adequate for the task? Is there enough time left to do the job?

Despite my misgivings, the compulsion to move forward will not relent. Completing this book, and attempting to get people to read it, is the beginning of my effort to confront those fears, and move on with my mission.

This manuscript represents a great deal of work over several years, but it is clearly imperfect. I have rewritten it several times, and each time I do, I find things to change and clarify. Even as I write these words, I know there are sections I could expand or do differently, and alternative ways of arranging the material that might make better sense to some people.

However, every day I see parents and children interacting poorly, and I yearn to show them a better way.

For reasons we will discuss, most of us are not receptive to unknown people telling us how to parent our child. I hope that this book will be a reference, and provide credibility as I seek to spread its message.

The more time I spend attempting to make the book perfect, the longer parents must struggle on without the opportunity to do better. I pray it is good enough. It's time for the message to be heard.

Table of Contents

Introduction

Parenting is likely the most important task we will ever undertake, yet surprisingly, it is generally approached in a curiously haphazard way.

Not having a clear method, or even a clear goal to give guidance for what to do in any given situation, we find ourselves relying mostly on memories and impressions of our childhood, searching for similar situations and copying what happened to us. Secondarily, we might ask the advice of family and friends.

Unconsciously, we emulate our neighbors, and to a surprising degree, we are directed by messaging from television, radio, the internet, and other mass media.

Occasionally we look to authority figures such as doctors, nurses, parenting coaches, and books.

If we have a goal, it is vaguely to teach our child “to be good”, or “what’s best”, or “what I know”, or “not to make the mistakes I made”.

All of this is completely normal, but as I will explain leads to generally sub-optimal and sometimes outright poor emotional, intellectual, and physical development in a child, and the waste of an opportunity for emotional and spiritual growth in a parent.

This is because the normal paradigm of parenting is to teach your child what you or others around you believe to be "true": Ignoring the fact that what we "know" and believe is based on the past; either our own or others', and may very well not be valid or useful in today's reality. (Things change!)

By forcing your child to accept as truth what is not, you shape them into a worldview that may or may not have been appropriate or adaptive for some past set of circumstances, but is almost certainly not optimal for the present in which they (and you) now live.

What I have discovered, and will show you in this book, is an alternative. You can parent your child in a way that fosters their adaptiveness, empathy, curiosity, and self-esteem, and avoids teaching incorrect beliefs that may later hinder their success and enjoyment of life. Simultaneously, this method will enhance your ability to emphatically connect with your child and others, and help you uncover and discard unconscious beliefs that are no longer helpful or appropriate for your current circumstances.

The elimination of false beliefs that hold you back from greater fulfillment, success, and happiness, leads to empowerment, and the ability to make positive changes in your life in multiple areas.

What exactly is this method? The crux of it is this: As much as possible, let your child take the lead. By establishing a strong empathic connection with your child, and then letting them take the lead as you both explore the world together, a magical process takes place which leads to a transformation in your perception of life, and the development of empathic empowerment in each of you.

The details of why this works, how to go about it, and other benefits that accrue to each of you, are the content of this book.

Practitioners of Transformative Parenting™ are in the happy position of having clearly defined goals for your child and yourself. For your child, our goal is to raise a happy, empathic, self-confident adult. For you, we wish to uncover and rectify false assumptions, about the world and yourself, and build your capacity for empathic understanding and communication.

By letting your child take the lead, you encourage happiness and self-confidence in your child and yourself. By modeling empathy, you teach empathy to your child, and become more empathic. Later in the book, I show these things more clearly, as well as how practicing this approach can teach us about ourselves and bring to light the false beliefs I mentioned.

In this aspect, Transformative Parenting™ is about freedom and awareness, how to obtain them for yourself, and preserve and secure them in your child.

While most directly addressing the needs of children, parents, and prospective parents, the knowledge in these pages is of great importance to everyone. Read it, even if parenting is the furthest thing from your mind. Indeed, read it before you start dating, and discuss your approach to childrearing with prospective mates before falling too deeply in love. This could save you a lot of conflict later.

As I will explain, in the course of living, and especially as we are growing up, we are all conditioned (trained, or programmed) by our experiences. Because of this conditioning, and because of how the mind works, we see the world only partially, necessarily incorrectly. We therefore interact with the world in overly limited, often incorrect ways. A core idea of Transformative Parenting™ is that we can enlist the aid of our child to identify and remove at least some of these learned impediments, while at the same time assuring that he or she is not subjected to the same limiting or incorrect programming.

This book will be very helpful for at least three groups of people: 1) the earnest parent, whose focus is strictly on assuring the optimal outcome for their child; 2) the spiritual seeker or mystic, who would like to understand how parenting can be approached as a spiritual practice, leading to personal transformation and higher consciousness; and 3) the psychotherapist or psychologist, looking for a fresh synthesis of psychological knowledge to help them better understand themselves and their patients.

If I had written separate books on psychological theory, spirituality and personal transformation, and parenting, I could have derived the core methodologies of Transformative Parenting™ in each of them. Instead, for completeness of understanding, and because each aspect relates to and supports the other, here all three approaches have been combined.

Despite my best efforts, many will find certain sections hard to read and understand. I apologize in advance. We all see the world differently, and have different backgrounds. Those who have training in psychological theory will find some parts of the book easier to read than those who lack that training. Similarly, those who have spent time on a spiritual path will find other parts of the book easier to understand. Finally, those who have previously raised or worked with children will relate most easily to some other sections.

Because it is such a rich and deep book, for full understanding you will likely need to read it more than once. I encourage you to use the first read to get a quick overview. The second read might be a bit more careful, perhaps highlighting points that are confusing as you go along. Finally, on the third read, take your time and try to understand everything.

God, or the Universe willing, there will be further opportunity to refine these explanations, and offer alternatives that will help the concepts be understood more easily by a wider audience. In the meantime, please persevere. The book is not as important as the ideas in it. Once you have understood the ideas, help the world by spreading them in the way that makes the most sense to you.

In an attempt to keep things understandable to everyone; not just specialists in psychology, child care, or meditation, I have defined my terms as I use them, proven my points with common-sense thought experiments, and provided lots of examples.

While this book abstracts and summarizes a lifetime quest for understanding, it is eminently practical, because it will have direct application in improving your life. You will learn to identify things that need to change, and ways of changing them.

Parenting, or child rearing, is perhaps the most important task any of us will ever undertake in terms of our ultimate impact on the future. However, parenting is devalued, to the point that most people approach it as an afterthought to their career, spouse, or their own pleasure. We believe it is possible for a parent to prioritize their own wants and needs, minimize or disregard their child's wants and needs, and still expect them to grow into a healthy, self-confident, compassionate adult. In general, unless you are lucky, and have a lot of good help, I think this perception is false. I point out the high levels of diagnosed attention-deficit disorders, autism spectrum disorders, anxiety disorders, and depressive disorders in children and young adults as evidence for my opinion.

Once understood, Transformative Parenting™ is simple, but it is not easy. It requires a primary commitment to your child, which leads in a synergistic way to your own self-growth.

This book is about parenting, and being a child, and finally about a way of being in the world which combines the knowledge of adulthood with the joy and wisdom of childhood. It outlines a path to that way of being for both the child and the parent.

However, this book is also about the implications of being human. Once you are able to observe your mind with some dispassion, it becomes clear that most of the traps we have fallen into as individuals, in relationships, in groups, and as a species, are logical consequences of how our minds operate.

I will explain to you simply and clearly how your mind and everyone else's mind works, so you can see this for yourself.

Thus, whether you are expecting to be a parent in the near future, the distant future, or not at all, you will find here a path to greater awareness.

If you are not planning to be a parent in the near future, your process in learning to overcome your conditioning will be somewhat different from the Parent's Path, which I am going to elucidate in some depth here, but I will give you a starting point, and some hints, to begin discovering your own Way.

This is not a religious book, though I occasionally share quotes from various religious traditions. While the subject can also be approached effectively from a religious or spiritual viewpoint, my explanations here are secular and rational. I hope this will allow the greatest number of people to accept the core ideas.

Parenting like life, is a living, dynamic system, impossible to describe fully in any book. If I had tried, the book would have become far too long to be readable, and the subject matter - however interesting and exciting in itself - would have become dull and pedantic. What I have done instead, is to provide a series of snapshots of the subject from various angles, in the hope you will be able to combine them into your own holistic synthesis.

Consider this Sufi story:

> *"An elephant is brought at night to a dark room.*
> *One by one, a series of people who have never seen an elephant are led into the room, and questioned when they return.*
> *One happens to touch the trunk, and describes a water-pipe kind of creature.*
> *Another, the ear. 'A very strong, always moving back and forth, fan-animal.'*
> *Another, the leg.'I find it still, like a column on a temple.'*
> *Another touches the curved back. 'A leathery throne.'*
> *Another, the cleverest, feels the tusk. 'A rounded sword made of porcelain.'*
> *He is proud of his description.*
> *Each of us touches one place and understands the whole that way.*
> *The palm and the fingers feeling in the dark are how the senses explore the reality of the elephant.*
> *If each of us held a candle there, and if we went in together, we could see it."*
> *- Rumi*

Like the characters in Rumi's parable about Reality, in each section of this book I talk about a particular aspect of Transformative Parenting™. I hope that as you read and ponder these various aspects of it, you will create an accurate internal image or model of the whole.

I have had to cut short many of the discussions, and hopefully what remains is enough. If concepts remain unclear, reach out to us on our website. The details are at the end of the book.

I have focused mostly on the first years of life, both from the view of a parent, and a child - because this is the time of greatest opportunity for both of you. I believe the methodology can be extended to later years, but that will be up to the diligent parent to work out for yourself as best you can, and certainly will be easier with the first few years of experience and practice behind you.

Transformative Parenting™ encourages us to perceive and value children as teachers as well as learners. This book explains why this is so vitally important, and how to go about it in a way that maximizes the benefits to you the parent, your child, and perhaps eventually humanity as a whole.

In the first chapter I provide a brief (as far as these things go), yet powerful understanding of the mind and its functioning. Among other things, I will demonstrate to you why your current worldview is incomplete and inaccurate.

Awareness of how your mind works allows you to take steps to counter the confusion and mistakes that come about when we operate from our usual place of "non-awareness". In particular, it will help you to be a more compassionate, aware, and understanding parent and human being.

In further chapters, we continue to weave the tapestry of Transformative Parenting™, with alternating discussions of parenting, transformation, and the mind. You will come to understand it as a path to enlightenment and self-awareness, in which your child helps you to understand yourself and the universe better - and as a path of parenting that seeks to minimize the faulty conditioning we otherwise unconsciously impose on our children, while encouraging the development of empathy and self-confidence.

We will consider why it is important to look at parenting as a two-way process, with our children teaching us as much or more as we teach them, and how to develop skills that enhance the practice of Transformative Parenting™ and our lives in general: Internal self-awareness and control, and empathic attunement to others.

Thank you for reading this book, and beginning the process of transformation that will allow you, and your children, to have richer, more authentic, more fulfilled lives.

A Perspective on Psychology

"Everything should be made as simple as possible, but not simpler."
– Albert Einstein

In college, my calculus teacher was a mysterious, imposing figure. He dressed in dark clothes, and always had a somber expression. He had a bad hand, I believe his left, which was always in a black leather glove and clenched in a fist. The fingers of that hand he never used, but he used the fist to clamp a book of matches, or pack of cigarettes against his body, which he would smoke before class as he considered what to teach us that day. He never carried notes or a book, but his lectures and demonstrations were delivered with infallible precision and logic.

He used to tell me: "If shipwrecked on a deserted island, a good mathematician should be able to recreate by himself the entire structure of mathematics." To paraphrase: Understand deeply whatever you do, so that you can prove the validity of what you say based on things you have experienced yourself. Be aware when you are relying on unproven hypothesis or opinion.

When you are finished reading this book, I would like you to be able to write a similar one on your own. I want you to have that deep an understanding of this approach. When you have that deep understanding, it is more likely that when you are confronted with a new or strange situation, you will be able to work out for yourself a creative solution that will allow for continued growth and realization for you and your child. In addition, you will be able to pass on that understanding to others.

It is also easier to have faith in something you understand deeply. In modern times it seems there are always conflicting opinions, indeed conflicting scientific studies, to be considered. If you have a solid foundation of understanding of any subject, in this case psychology and parenting, you will be able to stay the course, and not pulled willy-nilly by each conflicting voice you hear.

This chapter could be a separate book in itself. However, the material is very important for everyone to be aware of, and parents in particular. Please take your time going through it, and do your best to have patience with me, and yourself, and trust that in the end you will appreciate its importance.

I am going to pass on to you the essentials of how our minds work, as distilled by me after a great many years of training, education, experience, and thinking about psychology, psychiatry, and psychotherapy. I do this for two reasons:

First, the job of parenting is multifaceted. In order to understand how to be a parent, you must understand human beings, since both you and your child are human beings, and because you and your child need to learn how to best deal with other human beings. In order to understand human beings, you must understand yourself. In order to understand yourself, you must understand your mind, which is what creates your subjective experience of yourself and the world around you.

This psychological understanding will frame and give context to the ideas of Transformative Parenting™, which I will talk more about in later chapters. If you have previous knowledge of other psychological theories, I ask you to put critical judgment on hold for a while, until you have digested my discussion. I have altered the language of some theories to allow the ideas of many theories to be understood in a unifying context. Please try to keep your cup half-empty, and allow space for a fresh way of looking at things.

The second reason I offer this understanding of the mind, is analogous to why a farmer turns the soil before planting: To help make the soil receptive to the seed.

Many people have hardened views of reality, and parenting in particular. I am going to prove to you that no one's view of reality is correct. We all have flaws in our understanding of the world around us and the people and things in our environment. Once we realize that, a question arises for parents: How and what should we teach our children? I will give some answers here, and more in later chapters as our understanding of Transformative Parenting™ deepens.

Thoughts, Words, Labels, Objects

Let us start by considering how imprecise thought and communication are. As we go through this, note the many ways in which inaccuracies in our thinking arise from our limited perceptions, and how these inaccuracies are added to by the ways our minds process those perceptions.

In the same way that chemical compounds are formed from atoms, thoughts or sentences are made of words. And much as measuring the location and momentum of an isolated atom is imprecise, words in isolation are likewise imprecise. Words vary in meaning from person to person, and context to context.

For an example of this imprecision, let us take the word "car". There are an infinite number of things I might mean by this word, depending on the context: I could mean the letters: "c" "a" "r", if I was talking about the spelling. It could be the sound "kar" of the spoken word if I was talking about pronunciation. Alternatively, I might mean a particular car, in either your mind or mine, or the general class of things we might define as cars. When I say or hear the word "car", almost certainly my mental image of what that word represents for me at this moment, will be different from the image (or perhaps feeling, sound, or smell) which forms in your mind or is felt as a sensation in your body. The same is true for any word you care to state. (Prove that statement for yourself: Pause and consider if you can come up with a word that produces exactly the same mental image in someone else's mind as yours.)

In an attempt to reduce the ambiguity of isolated words, we put lots of them together to create a context. Indeed that is what I am attempting to do with this book. However, there are never enough of them.

As an example, when I evaluate a new patient, I ask for a personal history. Necessarily, that history is incomplete. The words a patient chooses to describe their history and symptoms can only imperfectly describe a small subset of their actual history. Often very important facts are omitted inadvertently, because there is only so much information that can be remembered, and only so much of that remembered information can be passed on verbally in the time we have. Because the information passed on to me is incomplete, my internal "picture" of that patient is incomplete, and thus incorrect.

Often we must make due with many fewer words than in a book. Notice how frequently we misconstrue text messages, email messages, voicemails, or online posts.

These are all illustrations of an important point:

Our personal understanding of the world is imperfect, incomplete, inaccurate, and different from other peoples' views of the world. As a result, our view of the world is inevitably in conflict with others' views.

This is inevitable, not just because we use words to communicate our ideas, but for many other reasons I am going to share with you.

Despite the problems, words are the best way we have of passing on knowledge and ideas. So, I am going to do my best to define some terms which will be useful in helping us understand the workings of the mind, and hope that the context of this chapter and the rest of the book will combine to give you a clear understanding of the situation.

"The beginning of wisdom is to call things by their proper name."
-Confucius

We begin by naming or defining some terms that will be useful for our work:

First, the words *tangible object* or *real object,* two phrases I will use interchangeably. When I do, I am asking you to imagine any particular object in your external environment, as experienced at a particular point in time. This object must exist independently of you, and you must be able to verify its existence based on observation with your senses. A particular car, sight, smell, or other person, experienced at a particular moment would be examples.

Derived from generalizing or abstracting from the experience of particular tangible objects are things we will call *inner objects.* These are things that we generally consider separate from ourselves, but are intangible, internally understood things such as numbers, words, memories, and ideas. We can group both internal objects and tangible objects together and speak of them all as just *objects.* For example, I can talk about the concept of addition, and my keychain, as both being objects. The keychain is a real object, and the concept of addition is an inner object.

Let us vaguely define *I* or *me* as that part of ourselves we identify as uniquely us. The part of ourselves that experiences the sensory inputs our bodies provide us. It remembers the experiences we have had in the past, fantasizes about the future, and can direct our bodies to take action. I or me is the all-important experiencer of life, the most important being in the universe - you.

Objectification

An extremely important concept for understanding the functioning of the mind is something I will call *objectification* or *modeling*[1]. Objectification is a foundational mental process which I believe underlies much of animal, and most particularly, human behavior. We engage in it constantly, though we are not usually aware of it. The reality of this process and the consequences of its operation are what much of this chapter is about.

I believe the basic ideas of objectification, though worded differently, would be agreed to as valid by most neuroscientists and indeed by most people generally, after reading the following explanations. However, to my knowledge the logical consequences of objectification have not been thought through in the way I have done here, and are vastly important to an understanding of human and animal behavior. These consequences also have direct and crucial application to parenting.

I ask you to consider, in slow motion, how we interact with a tangible object in our environment; say a coin in your hand. As you observe it, note that what you see is not the coin, but photons of light that have reflected off it. Those photons pass through your eye's cornea and lens, and strike the back of your retina. There the photons activate specialized neurons, which through a complex cascade of chemical events relays information to a part of the brain

---

[1] I will also sometimes use the word *modeling* in the sense of a person modeling or showing a certain behavior for another to observe and perhaps copy. Hopefully the context will make it clear if I am discussing an internal process or an external behavior.

called the visual cortex. The information from all the retinal neurons combines to form an internal image. This image in the visual cortex is mingled with the tactile input from your fingers or palm, relayed to your primary somatosensory cortex, emotional input from your limbic system, intellectual overlays from the cerebral cortex, and information from other parts of your brain, to form a composite internal representation of the coin.

This composite, held-within-your-brain model is what your mind is actually interacting with, considering, and deciding what to do about.

Once the decision is made, an equally complex chain of events takes place. Neuronal activity starts from the motor cortex, enlists the aid of the cerebellum, radiates through multiple axons in the spinal column to synapse with multiple motor neurons, which activate multiple muscles to do the action you decided: Say flipping the coin, handing it to a cashier, or putting it away in your pocket.

Even after you have put the coin away, you might continue to think about it if it was special in some way, or perhaps you will think about a related, abstracted form, like "money".

The basic idea of objectification is this: Generally, while going about our daily lives, we believe we are interacting with "real" people and things in our environment, but actually, we are not. Instead, we are interacting with mental models of them, which we have created, and to which we have assigned certain traits, qualities, capabilities, and feelings. Usually we are unaware of the difference, unless there is a problem or flaw in our model.

To be precise, I could call this type of inner model an "inner model of a tangible object" to differentiate it from "inner model of an abstract object", such as feelings, numbers, ideas or theories, but in general it is not necessary to do so, as our minds work with both types of inner objects in exactly the same ways. For easier readability, I will mostly lump them together and refer to both types of inner object models as: *inner objects*, or *inner object models*, or *object models*, or *inner models*, unless it is important to differentiate between the two types.

For each tangible or real object in our universe, we have created a corresponding internal object, a model, or simulation of that real object, which is what we actually interact with, unconsciously, most of the time. We *objectify* (create an internal object model for) everything in the world around us, including people and living things, hence the term objectification.

This is an extremely useful and necessary process, because it allows us to model our world and make sense of what goes on around us. We create inner models for everything in our universe: rocks, clothes, cars, planes, cell phones, etc. For each external object, we have assigned qualities such as mass, color, shape, texture, and particular capabilities.

Consider a pair of shoes. I might look at a pair of shoes, notice the shape of the toes, and decide they are too squared off or pointy for my taste. For better or worse, that is my primary impression of that pair of shoes. Another person might notice the color, and decide they are just right for the outfit he recently bought. A cobbler might be most interested in their workmanship, and how easily they might be repaired. A buyer for a department store might think about their cost of manufacture, and whether they fit with the rest of the line they are bringing out next year. Out of the myriad, actually infinite range of qualities available to any particular tangible object, we each choose a particular subset which forms our internal representation of it, based on our interests and prior experience. Thus, each of our object models is unique, and different from anyone else's.

As a result, we all experience the objects around us differently. And because of that, each of us experiences a different and unique reality.

As stated above, this creation of internal objects from our experience of external objects, and the unconscious use of the resulting internal objects to make decisions about how we interact with and think about external objects, is what I am calling objectification. I will also refer to it as modeling, learning, or conditioning. The term conditioning evokes the idea of an external event forcing the internal object building, but you should understand there is also an active internal mechanism, manifested in the desire to learn about, master and control our environment; which impels us to create inner object models even without external coercion.

While I have used an inanimate object as an example to illustrate my point, it is important to reiterate that the same process occurs most of the time when we think about people, other living things, and even ourselves. We objectify people and other living beings in exactly the same way as inanimate external objects. Over the years, we have developed internal models of our friends that enable us to predict what they are likely to do and feel in any given situation. We know from our models that our friends are likely going to be happy to see or hear from us, and so we are comfortable approaching them. We know from other models that our enemies are likely going to be antagonistic, and so we avoid them. We also have notions about ourselves and our capabilities, what we like and don't like, people we like and don't like, jobs we like and don't like, which are all based on inner models we have created, or been taught, about ourselves. I call these inner models of ourselves *self-objects.*

These models of the various beings and things in our lives serve an important purpose. They allow us to have a sense of order, predictability, and control. If our inner model of the sun did not reassure us that it would arise every morning, our fear that every night would be our last would be overwhelming. Our models tell us when our paychecks will be cut, when our rent is due, that winter will be followed by spring, that our friends or family will help us if we lose our jobs. In short, they allow us to live our lives without constant anxiety about basic survival.

The theory of objectification allows us to understand the fear and anxiety people with dementia experience: They are losing the ability to access and manipulate the object models that organize and give them control over their life experience.

Objectification then, is not a bad thing in itself. It is a necessary capability for the survival of any intelligent life form. Humans seem to be particularly good at building and referencing these models, to the point that it is our dominant mental process, and therefore unnoticed. It all happens so quickly we are not aware of it.

Because of this lack of awareness, to my knowledge the attributes of the objectification process that are necessary, yet cause errors and misunderstanding, have not been recognized either. Let us consider these now.

Association

Association is connecting object models together. In our minds, we combine two (or more) models and create a new model that consists of the combination. We make an unconscious assumption they should go together, though that assumption may be incorrect. Activating or experiencing one of the objects or circumstances triggers the expectation of the other, or even a whole series of objects (events, or ideas).

The classical example here is of Pavlov's experiments with ringing a bell before feeding a dog. After some repetition, the dog produced saliva after ringing the bell. The dog had been conditioned by experience to associate the ringing of the bell with eating, and its mind responded by starting the production of saliva even before being presented with food.

Association underpins all object model formation, and in effect, all learning. For example, in early life the sound of the letter 'A' is associated with the symbol 'A', which is then associated with the symbol 'a'. The same process is repeated for the letter 'B', the letter 'C', etc.. In addition, A is associated with B, B is associated with C, and so on, as we build the object called 'Alphabet' from objects called 'Letters'.

The strength of association, that is, how firmly the new object model is held together in the mind, is related to several factors, two of which are proximity, in space or time, and repetition. To continue our example above, when we learn the alphabet, we generally do it by singing the alphabet song, which places each letter in a particular order, right after each other both in internal visual space, and in auditory time. We then repeat the song over and over until it is memorized. In short order, hearing or seeing "s", invokes an echo in our minds: "t", and so on.

Association happens constantly, either consciously or unconsciously. It is how we create our personal universe, and the glue that holds our personal universe together. Certain things cause or are caused by other things. Over time, we learn and consolidate vast interconnecting chains of association, which allow us to model the external world with remarkable precision.

Association can be used consciously, as in studying for school, learning a song, or learning to swing a bat. It will also occur unconsciously, when listening to others talk, reading, or when exposed to advertising.

In the study of statistics, we learn there is a difference between correlation and causation. Though sometimes events are correlated because one causes the other, often in daily life that is not the case. Because of how the mind works, there will be an assumption of causation, when there is no direct connection between the two events. Non-causal correlated events can occur randomly, and sometimes there is a third (perhaps unknown) event that is the actual cause of both of the correlated events we are observing.

As an example, some people believe autism is caused by vaccinations. This is based on the experience of some that symptoms in their children began shortly after a vaccination. Although such a conclusion cannot be proved wrong in a particular case, from what I understand, statistical studies have shown that the level of correlation between the onset of autism and having a vaccination is within the level expected if they were unconnected with each other, or at least connected only by the common factor of early age.

Despite this logical explanation though, a particular parent whose child begins having autistic symptoms shortly after getting a vaccination will most likely feel there is a strong causative connection between the two events. We can understand this as a normal feeling once we understand the phenomena of unconscious association.

Emotions can be considered a type of inner object, and are almost always associated to other inner objects such as ideas, concepts, inner models of external objects, and other emotions.

Consider a child who is publicly humiliated in a math class, say when there were issues at home which precluded their putting in the study necessary to keep up. In mathematics this problem tends to compound itself as the subject matter builds in complexity, and it can be difficult to catch up, especially when subjected to ridicule, or in the face of poor supports at home or at school.

At that point, the path of least resistance may be for the child to associate feelings of helplessness and shame into their model of mathematics, give up on learning math, and be anxious evermore at the prospect of doing even trivial mathematical tasks; even though that person's natural mathematical ability may be no different from someone who enjoys doing math problems, and so does them a lot, and is therefore good at them.

In my professional practice and in informal life, I have frequently observed the chaining together of shame or embarrassment or other emotional pain to anger. Indeed, in my observation most people who have "anger issues" are actually quite insecure, and sensitive to emotional wounding. That wounding then triggers anger, which gives them a sense of control over the more painful emotions they are trying to avoid.

As I discuss in more depth later, the associations we make in early life are of utmost importance. As a baby, do we associate awakening with the presence of a soft touch, a calm reassuring voice, a juicy nipple, joy and contentment, or with rough handling, painful hunger, nasty smells, or fearful isolation? These early associations form the basis of our primary models of our parents, the world, and ourselves.

Incompleteness

Internal mental objects, as I mentioned above in the example of the pair of shoes, are derived from a subset of the attributes that the external object actually has, and are thus incomplete. The consumer of the shoes has one set of perceptions about them; the person on the assembly line who made them has another, the person who designed them another. None of these people really understands everything there is to know about those shoes. As a matter of fact, if we consider the situation carefully, we realize no one can know everything there is to know about any tangible object. Thus, whatever mental model of an external object we have created, it must be incomplete.

Just to drive the point home, whatever we may think we know about another person, we cannot know all there is to know about them. Actually, we do not even know everything there is to know about ourselves. We cannot even come close!

Incorrectness

Incorrectness in our inner object models comes about in two ways. First, because of the incompleteness noted above and secondly because of wrong information we have received about the object from trusted others.

Incorrectness because of incompleteness arises due to faulty inferences we draw from our incomplete knowledge of the object. For example, we might think the neighbor next door is a great guy because he smiles at us when we see him, invites us to his frequent parties, and he once shoveled a path through our sidewalk after a big snowstorm. What we do not know is that he has been embezzling large sums from the schoolteacher's pension fund for years. If we had this information, likely our opinion of him would change dramatically.

Another example is a piece of wood that looks good, but breaks when we walk up the stairs because it is rotted on the inside. Because of our incomplete knowledge of the wood, we trusted (wrongly) that it would support our weight.

When looked at a certain way, incorrectness of an object model due to wrong information from a trusted source is an extension of the case of incomplete knowledge: Our incomplete knowledge of the trusted source has led us to trust them, where they should not have been trusted. Relying on that trust, we incorporate their untrue statements about some other object into our inner model of that object. Let's look at some examples.

Santa Claus

In this myth, which is commonly celebrated in the United States and many other countries, an omniscient, extremely powerful older man brings presents to children once a year on the anniversary of Jesus' birth. If you have been a "good" child, you will get many presents, but if you have been "bad", you may not get any, or only a lump of coal. (A therapist I know actually had a patient who was given only a lump of coal in her stocking as a child.) This myth is generally believed by children up until the age of five or so, when many kids start to figure out one way or the other that what they have been told is untrue, and "Santa" is actually a collection of relatives, friends, and strangers dressed up in a red suit and a fake beard.

Here, children are led by trusted authority (parents), with the collusion of mass media and merchandise retailers, to believe that Santa is a real object (person), when in fact, he is not.

On its face, this seems like a fun deception for everyone. Parents have some leverage before Christmas to manipulate their children into being "good", meaning do as they are told. They get to see the joy on their children's faces when they open their presents, and children get their presents.

However, there are some problems here: To begin, there is the eventual revelation for children that they have been lied to by their parents. As I explain later, it is very important that children be able to trust their parents absolutely, and this lie, though told with generally good intentions, puts a question in their child's mind: What else have my parents lied to me about?

Another issue is that parent's endorsement of the mass media deception lends unconscious credibility and trust to other mass media and merchandising events, and likely enhances the influence of mass media and retail messaging on the individual throughout later life.

This myth also teaches that the reason for good behavior is to obtain material reward. This implies both that material things are essential for happiness, and that good people have more material things. Since the Santa Claus myth also conflates, or mixes the idea of an omniscient God with

Santa Claus, it therefore creates the impression that wealthy people must be "good" (because God favors them), and conversely that poor people must be "bad".

This conditioning has impacts later on. An investment banker, who found himself shocked at the behavior of his boss, once related to me how amazed he was to observe how many people mistakenly believe those who have wealth are "good people", and can be trusted! Conversely, how many times have you heard the opinion that people are poor because they are lazy, or into drugs, or lack faith?

What you as a parent will choose to do about this issue will be your decision. To be honest with you, our child still believes in Santa, out of deference to tradition on both sides of the family.

If your family does "do Santa", consider minimizing the "good" and "bad" child gets "lots" or "no" gifts message, and consider not adding your trusted voice to perpetuating the illusion. Others will do that for you. I often tell my daughter: "that's what people say", instead of affirming with certainty that Santa lands on the roof and climbs down the chimney for example.

Consider also looking up the story of St. Nicholas, and telling your child the truth; that this is a tradition about giving to those in need, which honors a very nice person who lived a long time ago. And still give them some nice gifts on Christmas Day.

The False Witness

Not uncommonly, someone (often a teenager) decides to "have some fun" and spreads a lie about another person. Perhaps to get back at the victim for some presumed slight, or perhaps just to reinforce their role as a leader of their social group. This can have tragic consequences for the picked-on individual, as likely we have all experienced either directly or from observation.

Here, the other individuals in the social group have mistakenly given trust to the ringleader, and also mistakenly believed something untrue about the victim. Therefore, the internal object models that represent the ringleader and the victim are both incorrect.

The Scam Artist

It should be pointed out that we all become scam artists of a sort when we believe another scam artist, and then act to try to get someone else to believe as well. While the true scam artist uses fake sincerity to convince us of what he or she is selling or trying to get us to do, once we are convinced, our real sincerity leads us to do just as much damage or more to those around us. Unwitting victims refer many of those harmed by Ponzi schemes to the organizer.

It is useful to remember the admonition of my calculus teacher to understand deeply why you are doing something, and not accept it simply because of some other person's presumed authority. A healthy skepticism is useful, and is to be encouraged in most cases, both in others and ourselves. Often the result of independent study and reflection will agree with the statements of authority figures, but sometimes they will not.

Rigidity

It is a characteristic of mental models that once formed they resist change, sometimes despite strong evidence that the model is incorrect. I am calling this resistance to change, rigidity. In common psychological parlance this is called *resistance*. You could also conceptualize it as a psychic form of inertia.

Rigidity has an important positive function, in that it allows us to feel secure in our knowledge, and hence reduce our feelings of anxiety about the unpredictability of the world around us. However, sometimes the evidence of the world and our inner model of the world are in conflict. This conflict can cause a great deal of anxiety, or be expressed as anger, depression, or multiple other ways. It is most helpful to be able to identify inner models that are in conflict, and be open to changing them, to better fit new evidence.

Unfortunately, the ability to calmly and consciously recognize when our inner models and our outer experience are in conflict, without personalizing the event (see next paragraph), requires a high degree of self-awareness which we are rarely able to sustain for long. Part of the purpose of this book is to give you the tools to be more self-aware, which will allow you to refine and adapt your inner object models more easily and thus become less conflicted with both your internal and external world.

Identification

An important aspect of rigidity is a phenomenon I am going to call identification, or *personalization*. That is, we identify ourselves with our object models. We see this often in arguments. We disagree about some characteristic of an object, but instead of approaching the issue calmly, we get angry, because we identify ourselves with our inner model of that object.

In identification, when someone disagrees with your model, they are not only disagreeing with your model, they are disagreeing with you, meaning your whole being.

We feel disagreement to be an implicit rejection or disapproval of our entire being, which arouses emotions such as anger or sadness. This aspect of objectification is responsible for much unnecessary conflict and suffering in the world, and again I am hopeful I can help you discover a level of self-awareness that will protect you to some extent from being trapped in this dysfunction.

I say dysfunction, because as you remember, it is impossible to not be in conflict with others about our inner object models. We all operate with limited information, sometimes wrong information about the world around us. We all have had unique life experiences, and so of necessity we all have different inner models of the objects that make up our world. As a result, if we are able to be honest with each other, we will all have differences of opinion about everything.

Unless we are very careful and aware, disagreement, which is inevitable, can transform into violence; either verbal or physical, in a misguided attempt at "self-defense" where self-defense was not actually necessary. You see this often in political and sports discussions, where seemingly meaningless disagreements (to an outsider) can explode into violent confrontation.

Again, because we rely on the validity of our object models to protect us from fears of death, isolation, oblivion, and chaos, we strongly resist attempts to modify them. Identification is part of the defensive response that resists change to our internal models.

Abstraction

In abstraction, several inner object models are combined into a single version. In contrast to association, where object models are chained together in their entirety, in abstraction common traits are noted in several object models, and only these common traits are combined into a new model. When I talked about the word "car" earlier, what was recalled by your mind may well not have been the image of any particular car, and certainly not an inner video of all the cars you've ever seen, but a "gestalt" or "sense" of what a car is, based on your observation of many cars. In a similar way, the concept of a number, say "3", is an abstraction based on observations of many groups of three things.

This creation of abstracted versions of objects can be very useful, because it allows us to make predictions about any similar object we encounter in our environment. Say we are walking across the street and see a car coming down the road. Based on past experience, we are able to predict with some precision that it will take a certain amount of time to reach us, or cause a certain amount of injury if it were to collide with us at its current speed, despite the fact we may never have seen that particular car before. Our abstracted models of car, mass, and velocity allow us to do that.

This abstraction process is what is involved in theorizing and hypothesizing. It is how our minds create the idea of numbers for example; abstracting from groups of tangible objects in our environment. Moreover, it is how we create all the other purely abstract mental objects we think about: like equations, rules of logic, or concepts like good and evil.

Projection (Combining Abstraction and Association)

Theorizing and hypothesizing have taken humanity quite a long way in our ability to better control our environment, but there can be big problems when we unconsciously substitute our abstracted versions of objects for particular real objects. This occurs frequently, particularly when we are on autopilot and preoccupied with something else.

For example, we may be driving down a road we have driven so many times we hardly need to think about it, and so we don't. I have many times arrived home from a destination without actually remembering much of the drive. Especially on an interstate highway, our minds can allow us to think about something else, substituting an abstracted version of "highway" so we hardly have to look at the road.

This is fine until something happens that is out of the ordinary. We come upon a new hole in the road, or someone stops unexpectedly in front of us. Then the discrepancy between the abstracted inner model and the real object becomes potentially dangerous.

This substitution also occurs when we are interacting with people, and is the cause of racial, religious, socio-economic, or educational prejudice. We have constructed or learned an abstract model of "Christian" or "Jew" or "Muslim", or "White" or "Black" or "Asian" or "Latino", or "Man" or "Woman" or whatever. When we meet someone who belongs to one of our abstract categories, we immediately project (see below) or associate our abstracted model onto them, and find ourselves having certain expectations of them as a result. This happens unconsciously. The problem is that most of our abstracted models about groups of people are formed and projected without our realizing it, and frequently turn out to be quite inaccurate when tested against experience with individuals in the group, or even just studied consciously. Other words for this mental activity are stereotyping, and generalizing.

In projection, an abstracted mental image, or model, along with its corresponding associated traits, is associated with or assigned to a real object instead of evaluating the object freshly as itself.

(Actually, we are associating the abstracted object to our inner object model of the particular real object or person. However, as a kind of shorthand, and in deference to standard psychological parlance, we speak of projecting the abstracted model *onto* the real object.)

We project an abstracted route home onto the current day's trip instead of paying attention to our driving. We project "homeless person", "drug addict", or "bum" onto the person sleeping under newspapers in the park instead of bothering to consider them as unique human beings.

Projection (short for "projection of abstracted inner model") occurs constantly. Whenever we encounter someone or something in our environment or our imagination, our mind does its best to find previously learned abstracted models we can associate with it.

Projection allows us to make predictions about behaviors and characteristics that are generally helpful to us in navigating our world. However, since projection is going on constantly, we rarely look at anyone or anything with a "fresh eye". This saves us time and energy, but is often misleading.

Let us take as an example a woman who has a bad day at work and leaves feeling persecuted by her boss and peers. The self-object of "persecuted", is activated. She leaves work, comes home, and finds her daughter has not cleaned her room as expected. She flies into a rage, believing her daughter has done it maliciously to torment or persecute her. The "persecuted" self-object or model, demands the presence of a real persecutor. Feeling persecuted, but lacking the presence of an actual persecutor, her mind found a substitute. She projects the role of persecutor onto her daughter.

Hopefully, when she calms down she will realize this is not a likely motivation at all. Forgetfulness, or even a stubborn attempt at autonomy and independence, are reasonable possibilities, but malicious persecution is not likely.

Our minds are primed, by emotion or previous conditioning, to expect or look for certain objects in the world. That is, we look for an external object that fits our internal expectations. When we find an external object that might possibly be a match for what we expect, we associate or "project" the internally expected object onto the found real object. This assignment of the expected internal object model to the real object is sometimes appropriate, and sometimes not.

Self-Projection

Sometimes the attributes of a self-object (part of our beliefs about "me" or "I") are incorrectly assigned to an external person or thing.

Often the initial trigger is that some part of "me" experiences a desire or emotion that other parts of "me" are uncomfortable with or reject. This feeling or desire persists nonetheless, and so the mind searches for an object to associate it with. In this case, an inner object that represents an external person will be the most likely, but it can also be an external animal or thing. Sometimes, the mind will struggle mightily to find an appropriate object, and in the end will use the slightest pretext to justify attaching the label to the best (external) candidate it can find, rather than applying it to oneself.

For clarity, I call this self-projection. This is the form of projection most commonly discussed in psychological literature, though here it is only a subset of the broader function of projection.

An example might be a driver who is hurrying home in rush hour, and has been cutting in and out of lanes attempting to get ahead of the general flow of traffic. He is suddenly cut off by another driver changing lanes ahead of him, (who may not have even seen him because he was moving from lane to lane so quickly) and flies into a rage at the other driver for being reckless and risking an accident. Here, it is uncomfortable for the man to accept that he himself has been reckless, and so he projects that attribute onto the other driver.

Self-projection is quite prevalent. I believe it accounts for the behavior of "Tiger" parents, and abusive parents who have themselves been abused. They are projecting parts of their own self-models (insecurity, and "badness" respectively), onto their children. Some hunters project malevolence or evil onto the "varmints" they kill.

Although these are extreme examples, I believe most parents interact with their children primarily through the process of self-projection. That is, they are teaching their children to be like themselves (or perhaps idealized versions of themselves, see below).

Projection is also present in more subtle forms, such as the pleasure we have when we look at a photograph of a loved one, or when we smell a scent that reminds us of a pleasant time in our lives. We find that we "like the photograph", or "like the scent", when really the photograph might be an old, grainy, beaten up black and white, and the scent not that remarkable in itself. We associate abstracted pleasant feelings with the image in the photograph, or the scent of our beloved.

Idealization

A particularly powerful type of projection is idealization. Here, a highly positively-regarded abstract mental object or model (an ideal) is projected, making the person or object projected onto highly regarded. There are many examples, such as money, power, beauty, musical ability, or even holiness being projected onto particular people. (The projection of a highly negatively-regarded abstract model we call *demonization,* and works the same way as idealization.) The dilemma here, as with all projection, is that you do not perceive the person, but regard them primarily as whatever you have idealized them to be.

Falling in love is a particular form of idealization, which keeps us from seeing our loved one's faults. There are also times when we project love onto someone, and we are unable to perceive that the person "underneath" the projection actually does not love us. This can be the case with stalkers, or delusional fans for example.

Children idealize their parents. Power, trust, love, beauty, actually everything; including negative traits such as hatred, anger, and pain are contained in the early idealization of parents by their children. Another way of saying this is that parents carry the projection of the early God image. If you are religious, this means that for your young children you are God's proxy (substitute or stand-in), in other words you are God to them. How you relate to your child now will strongly determine the type of relationship they have with

God later. If you are not religious, how you relate to your young child now will strongly determine the types of relationships they have with authority figures, other people, and even their universe as a whole later on in life.

Projective Identification and Interpersonal Manipulation

Suppose the angry driver in the example above decides to aggressively pass the driver who inadvertently cut him off; honking, and "giving him the finger" as he does so. In this situation, it would be reasonable for the second driver to feel under attack. He may in response become angry himself, and seek ways to attack the first driver, perhaps by cutting him off at the next opportunity. He has been induced to become the reckless driver the first driver perceived him to be.

Projective Identification begins with receiving or noticing the projection of another person (often unconsciously), this triggers the activation of a self-object model in the perceiver, which then induces a behavior matching the original projection. You become what the other person expected you to be.

This process often occurs in subtle ways. A woman enters an elevator, which holds another woman. The first woman notices a certain look in the eye, a glance away, a body posture that is interpreted as saying "I don't want you here." The first woman then feels rejected, shifting to anger. Her spine straightens, and her stare becomes cold. The second woman notes this shift in posture, and reacting similarly assumes a standoffish posture and mental attitude. She has become what the first woman assumed she was, perhaps without a word being spoken. Such "first impressions" can be very difficult to correct later, especially because these non-verbal communications are rarely talked about, or even consciously noted.

In classical psychological literature, projective identification is generally limited to the case of an unconscious projection of a self-object (as with the car driver). However, within our framework it can be understood as part of a more broadly experienced process; which can be, and is, used consciously by those who are skilled in interpersonal manipulation. With developing awareness and understanding, you will see the process occurring in interactions with friends, family, teachers, marketers, salespeople, governments, and cultures, used either consciously or unconsciously to modify and control your behavior.

We call the conscious use of projective identification interpersonal manipulation (or *marketing*, or *salesmanship*).

Sophisticated techniques have been developed to cause you to associate a given product, belief, or idea with one or more positively regarded self-object models (branding in marketing terminology). Then, when that self-object model is activated, it will trigger the purchase of the associated product, or reinforce the belief or idea. This is done consciously by salespeople, marketers, and politicians, and mostly unconsciously by ordinary people in day-to-day interactions.

Here is an example:

You are driving down the highway, or riding on the subway. You see an image on a billboard, or a subway car ad showing a happy, good-looking, well-dressed man, surrounded by beautiful women gazing lovingly or passionately at either him, or the glass of liquor he his holding. There is an image of the bottle, with the brand prominently displayed, and optionally a written message reinforcing the idea that beautiful women are strongly attracted to men who drink that particular brand of liquor.

By simply viewing that advertisement, the idea of drinking that brand of liquor is unconsciously associated with the self-object models of being happy, good-looking, successful, sexually attractive, and being socially popular. If the target of the advertisement, in this case a liquor-drinking, heterosexual male, finds himself in a situation which activates one of these models, or where he wants to activate one of these models, then barring other influences he will order the advertised liquor if it is available. After doing so, he will find himself feeling happier, better looking, more successful, more sexually attractive, and more socially comfortable, independent of the neurological effects of the liquor. The drink has served as a *trigger* or *anchor,* to activate or reinforce the desired self-objects (self-beliefs) to which it has been associated.

The self-object model of being sexually attractive is often utilized for this purpose. Everything from cigarettes to cars to liquor to farm machinery, and probably every imaginable product there is, has been associated to this self-object model in a frequently effective attempt to sell the product or idea.

Being socially desirable is a more general, yet equally powerful self-object model that is exploited for interpersonal manipulation or projective identification. In other words, the self-idea you are (or want to be) a good person, esteemed, respected, powerful, or nice to be around, can be used to manipulate you. The power of peer pressure, the desire to adhere to social norms, as well as the stability of group religious and cultural practices, can be explained by the drive to be socially connected.

I will talk more about innate drives later, in a chapter I have devoted to that subject, but for now note that the drive to be socially connected can be derived from the fear of death. From birth, we recognize that alone we cannot survive; we need help from other people - hopefully our loving parents. Thus, the powerful instinct to belong to a group can be seen as a normal outcome of the instinct to live - since belonging to a group is required for our survival.

The combination of messaging, which states you will enjoy social connectedness if norms are followed, and you will be socially outcast if you do not, creates a powerful pressure to adhere to group-approved behavior. If you follow the social norms of your group, the desirable inner self-models of being socially connected, admired, respected and liked are triggered and reinforced. If you act in a way that is unacceptable to your group, the inner self-model of being outcast is activated, which creates anxiety and discomfort. This explains many aspects of group behavior, including "mob psychology", where individuals do things they ordinarily would not, when faced with the choice of social connectedness or being ostracized or even physically harmed. Extreme self-object models such as murderer, killer, or avenger, which exist in all of us but are ordinarily suppressed by cultural messaging, can become activated when required by a group with which we strongly identify.

Relative Validity

Validity is a measure of the "correctness" of an object-model. How well does the object-model correspond to the real object on which it is based? Due to incompleteness and incorrectness, an object-model is never totally valid in all contexts. However, object-models all have a level of relative validity, based on their usefulness in prediction of events. Remember, a model, which is valid relative to a particular context, is not necessarily valid in another. Times change, and circumstances change.

An example which comes to mind is of a friend who for a while after returning from Vietnam, would drop flat on his face and scurry for cover at the sound of an engine backfiring. His object models of appropriate survival activities, associated to his models of "gunfire", "artillery", "grenade", or "land mine" objects, which were associated with similar sounds, were perfectly valid and appropriate while he was in combat, but no longer valid or acceptable in civilian life. Social customs which are valid in one culture and incorrect in others, such as differing attitudes towards eye contact, hand shaking, and bowing, are examples of culturally defined object-models of polite behavior which are relatively valid in one context but may not be in others.

It has been my observation as a psychotherapist, that almost all of us are burdened with object models that were relatively valid at an earlier point in our lives, but are no longer useful or valid in our current life context. Discovering these, and minimizing their effects, is an important part of effective psychotherapy. It is also an important part of Transformative Parenting™.

Awareness

Understanding these foundational mental processes is an important first step to gaining some objectivity about your world and your place in it. Unfortunately, reading about and even understanding objectification (which is simply adding more object models to your repertoire), is not enough to free you from their negative effects. For that we also need awareness, the ability to recognize when these events are occurring within ourselves and others as they happen. A skilled psychotherapist can help, but here is a tip to help you become more aware on your own: note the arising of strong negative emotion (fear, anger, depression). When these negative emotions arise, it is because of a strong conflict in two or more of your inner object models. If it is not an emergency, seek to discover what the internal conflict is, as opposed to acting out an imaginary conflict with an external object (person or thing) onto whom you are likely projecting your inner conflict.

By monitoring your negative emotions, and using them as a signal for the need for self-reflection, instead of "acting out" immediately, you become aware of problematic internal programming, which is necessary as a first step for change. In this book, I will be giving many examples of using this technique with parent-child interactions, but it can be applied fruitfully to adult-adult interactions as well. You will find that often the issue is faulty assumptions about other people's knowledge or states of mind, or others' faulty assumptions about your knowledge or state of mind.

It may helpful to first observe issues with faulty object models in friends and acquaintances, by watching arguments or heated conversations. Look to add to the examples I have given. (However, I suggest keeping your observations to yourself!) Seeing things in others is often easier than discovering things in us. Also, look for your own faulty object models. Those connected to yourself especially.

Though you should prove it for yourself, I think you will come to realize we are all the unique product of a lifetime of conditioning.

Through my work with thousands of patients, and my own psychoanalysis and self-reflection, I have concluded there is precious little about me or others that cannot be explained by taking into consideration two things: Inheritance, and life experience. Inheritance includes things like one's age, one's inherited wealth and influence, and traits such as hair color, skin color, eyesight, hearing, height, weight, intelligence, aggressiveness, and many other things that are given a certain weight by genetics. Inherited traits are modified; enhanced, or suppressed, by our life experience. Knowledge and beliefs on the other hand, are entirely dependent on what we have been taught; by either education or life experience.

Every one of us is the product of circumstance. The circumstance of our inheritance and the circumstance of our life experience. We all think, act, and react to everything around us based on just those two factors. If there is a small sliver or awareness of an unconditioned, primal "me" in each of us, it is almost entirely obscured by the impact of our inheritance, and identification with our unique basket of inner object models, which were created entirely in response to our experiences.

Understanding these things has enhanced my compassion for those who are less fortunate, or seem misguided, or dysfunctional, or with contrary opinions to my own. After all, they are acting rationally, as best they can, based on their inheritance and the results of their experience, just as we all are.

> *"There, but for the grace of God, goes John Bradford."*
> *- John Bradford, as he watched a fellow prisoner being led to the gallows.*

Once, my four year old was sitting in my lap when she turned and asked me with a smile: "Who are you?"

She was at an age where she clearly knew me as her Daddy. She knew I was a doctor, and had patients I treat because I like to help people. She knew my name. She knew that I love her and protect her above all else, and that I do my best to explain truthfully and to the best of my ability whatever she has questions about. So, I decided to answer her honestly, and said: "I don't know".

It is a curious thing to have the realization after many years of self-study, meditation, psychoanalysis, and psychological training that you do not know who you are. Yet, perhaps that is the logical outcome of the realization that "I" am entirely a product of my inherited genetics, and the experiences I have had. What is uniquely "me" beyond my genetics and the thoughts and memories that are a product of my experiences, I can only guess about.

While the discovery that your sense of who you are is wholly determined by your experiences and chance inherited factors can be unnerving and cause for initial confusion, it is also the opening of a door to freedom. Along with the anxiety of perhaps having to choose a new direction, your options in life widen dramatically.

My hope is that you will use what you have learned in this chapter to open a small crack in the walls of your accumulated conditioning, which surround you and limit your perspective and actions. Over time, and with continued effort, that crack will open wider, and allow you to rediscover that overshadowed, overlooked aspect of consciousness which is free, open, and joyous; yet filled with awe, reverence and gratitude.

If you are a parent, I hope you will use this understanding to become more aware of the conditioning experienced by your child, and do your best to minimize the creation and reinforcement of false real object models, or negative and limiting self-object models.

I will have more to say in later chapters about how the mind works, widening the door to awareness, choosing a meaningful path, and minimizing adverse conditioning in your child. For now, let us end with some summary thoughts. Thank you for hanging in there!

Takeaway Points

What we experience as an objective reality is actually almost entirely subjective. When we relate to an external object, most often we are actually relating to our inner model of that object.

Because of differing experience and genetic makeup, and because our internal models can never completely describe an external object, we all form unique internal representations (inner object-models) of the external objects around us.

Because the external world is constantly changing, and our inner object-models are incomplete, there is always some degree of incorrectness in our internal models of external people and things.

Due to the above factors, our models always differ in some ways from other people's models.

We create models of ourselves, as well as other people. (Moreover, we believe those models *are* ourselves and others.) These models are also incomplete and incorrect.

Disagreement with other people's object models often leads to anxiety, grief, conflict, anger, and violence, despite the fact that such disagreement is inevitable (because our object-models always differ).

Because of the properties of object model creation and access, we can be induced into behaving in certain ways without our conscious awareness.

Understanding these things leads to increased compassion for ourselves and others, reduced feelings of anger and hatred, an ability to defend against psychological manipulation, and the growing awareness of the possibility of psychic freedom.

A Perspective on Parenting

From the time a child is born, and even from the womb, he or she is creating, developing, and refining inner object models of the world around them, their inner states, and their sense of "I" or "me".

My hope is that by the time you are an adult and ready to become a parent, you will have acquired enough positive, relatively-valid object-models to allow you to function comfortably in society and feel fulfilled and happy. In addition, before becoming a parent, you will have anticipated and allowed for the additional stress of having a child on your financial position, social activities, and free time.

For most people facing parenthood though, this is not reality. Likely, we are not making enough money to be comfortable, much less comfortably add on the expense of a child. Likely, we are stressed on a daily basis by co-workers, clients, friends, and family who all seem to make incessant demands on our time. We have relationship issues, which create emotional conflicts that often seem insurmountable. We have dreams and aspirations that have never been fulfilled, and because of the demands on our time and limited resources, we may never be able to fulfill. Then, perhaps due to social pressure, biological drive, loneliness, or unhappy accident, we have a child; which of course adds to our list of problems.

Is it any wonder that many children, growing up in an environment filled with stress and conflict, absorb that stress and conflict and grow up being conflicted, anxious, unhappy and dysfunctional adults? In addition, I believe the current, normative style of parenting only exacerbates the situation, both for a child, and a parent, by putting unnecessary stress on each of them.

In the normative model of parenting, a child quickly becomes just another object in the parent's world that needs to be managed. After an initial wondrous period as a newborn, where a child receives the benefit of the parent's undivided attention and love, the parent transitions to focusing more and more on their pre-existing cares and concerns, and how to fit the new child-object into their life.

In addition, there are new social pressures to consider: What will neighbors, friends, and family think about them as a parent? Is the child being "well cared for"? Are they wearing proper clothing, eating proper food, being weaned at the proper time, being potty trained at the proper time, not using a pacifier, talking at the right time, walking at the right time, sharing with friends, not watching TV, being disciplined, being respectful, going to church, etc., etc.?

Under these circumstances, with so many expectations placed upon them, it is no wonder that a parent begins to consider their child as an object to be manipulated and managed. In fact, to some extent it is necessary to do so, because only by manipulating mental objects in our imaginations can we come up with solutions to the external problems of day to day living.

The problem is not that we have a mental model of our child; it is that we are unable to "turn it off". We equate our child with our model, which, because our child is "real", as I have explained earlier, can only represent a small subset of what our child actually is.

Additionally, what makes humans (and likely other sentient beings) special is that they contain within themselves their own universes of inner object models. Moreover, children are special, because their universes are in the early stages of developing and taking form.

The early years of childhood are when basic, foundational concepts of a child's universe and themselves are being formed. These primal inner object models are the ones on which all the others will be based. Am I safe here? Am I wanted? Am I loved? Am I understood? Am I respected? Am I powerful? Is this a happy place where I can enjoy myself and explore freely? If the answer to these questions is positive from early childhood, a child can feel comfortable, powerful, happy and content, which becomes their baseline sense or inner model of him or her self. With this secure base, it is much more likely that your child will develop into a calm, confident, self-assured adult.

When building a house, what comes first is the foundation. If the foundation is strong, the rest of the house can be strong. If the foundation is weak, it will be impossible to build a strong house.

In the normal way of parenting, the parent is trying to get their child to conform as quickly as possible to socially accepted norms of behavior. In addition, it is helpful if the child is "advanced" from their peers, because this means the parents are doing a superior job of training their child. The child should be walking, talking, out of diapers, not using a pacifier, not using a bottle or breast-feeding as soon as possible. They should be comfortable sharing, and sitting quietly, and above all should "do as they're told" when a parent or other adult directs them.

Unfortunately, this common approach is quite likely to cause children to create inner models of themselves that reflect the evidence they have; that they are powerless, have no autonomy, and are wanted and loved only if they obey without question the edicts of their parents or other adults. Moreover, they often learn they are intrinsically defective because they are unable to meet unreasonable expectations of behavior "like other children".

So how and why did this dysfunctional method of child rearing arise, and what keeps it in place?

One reason it persists is that we all have the tendency to recapitulate with our children the events of our own childhood. We all consider ourselves well-adjusted, knowledgeable people. We all "know" our points of view are the correct ones. Wanting the best for our children, we want them to be like us, and so consciously or unconsciously, we attempt to repeat our own childhood experiences with our children. We become our mothers or fathers to our own children. Any deviation from how we were raised feels uncomfortable, and requires conscious effort to maintain.

Why did the standard method arise in the first place? I believe the answer is that for millennia, the majority of humankind has lived in an environment of scarcity, and/or rigid social constraint.

When resources are scarce, children must be utilized to aid in the business of survival. They must be trained to work or scavenge, and as soon as possible. In such an environment, a child must be considered an object, to be molded as quickly as possible to a predefined, resource-producing model. Otherwise they will use up scarce resources, potentially threatening the survival of the family or group. Similarly, when there are rigid social constraints in a society, class, clan, or religious group, there are severe negative consequences to a family in which one of its members does not conform. In this situation also, a child must be molded to a predetermined norm, which at the least limits their potential development in multiple areas. It can also lead to severe feelings of shame and inadequacy when they have strong desires or drives in unacceptable areas. For example, if a person is genetically homosexual but is living in a homophobic or homo-antagonistic culture.

In light of the foregoing, it is humbling to consider that only now, in the postindustrial era, after millions of years of social evolution, is a significant portion of humanity in a position of relative security and freedom, which might allow it to embrace an entirely new paradigm of parenting. One which is not based strictly on the needs and wants of parents and society, but is instead focused primarily on nurturing the uniquely unfolding individual child, to maximize their inner potentials, and chance of living a life of fulfillment and happiness.

To discover how to best put these ideas into practice, let us consider some additional aspects of early childhood.

A child comes into the world with several inborn traits (part of our common genetic inheritance) which must be considered in any theory of parenting. First, is a sense of fear or anxiety. This is evident from a child's first cry. A child is flooded in early life with an overwhelming shock of lights, sounds, movements, tactile sensations, and inner sensations, which were either not present, or very much muted in the womb. There is as yet no context, or inner model of the world, which would allow him or her to feel secure, and so there is a primary fear. What as adults we might call the fear of oblivion, of being alone in a chaotic world. From the beginning, a child is aware of their powerlessness and utter dependency.

This fear, fortunately, has an antidote: The loving care of their parent. A child's experienced fear is greatly alleviated by being gently held, fed, spoken to softly, gently rocked, kept physically comfortable, given moderate, comfortable levels of stimulation, and opportunities to discover their new world. Essentially, feeling safe; and knowing they belong with a powerful, understanding protector.

When fear and anxiety are alleviated, and a child is comfortable and alert, they can be seen to be regarding the world around them in the most wondrous way. We can perceive through them the wonder of a colorful toy, or the sparkle of dust in a sunbeam, or the play of shadows on the wall, or the texture of mother's hand or breast. We can also feel their joy in these observations. They experience the miracle of existence in a fresh, open way, which is refreshing for us as well.

Especially as their ability to move independently in the world increases, there is apparent a sense of curiosity. Their minds, wanting to explore and discover, seek patterns and novel information about the world around them. If they have the support of a patient, loving, available, and attuned parent or caretaker, their fears are allayed; allowing them to make amazing discoveries of their powers of movement and their ability to control the world around them.

If all goes well, there can ensue a wonderful period of seeming omnipotence for a child, in which the universe is perceived as limitless, wondrous, and seemingly under their control, and where they are loved and supported by an all-powerful, all-knowing being or beings (their parents). It is my contention that if these observations are allowed to become part of the earliest, fundamental inner object models of their universe and themselves, they are very likely to perceive the world and themselves in a positive, empowered way throughout their lives.

Of course, at some point the requirements of the world supersede, and it becomes apparent that we are not omnipotent. However, it is my firm belief that most of us have been too conditioned from too early an age to focus too much on our limitations and shortcomings, and as a result, we limit our potentials and ourselves unconsciously and unnecessarily. Later, when we become parents, we then pass on those unnecessary limitations and shortcomings to our children, not even aware we are doing so, since we are not aware of them in the first place.

In Transformative Parenting™, we seek to establish this period of seeming omnipotence as early as possible in early childhood, allowing it to be as complete as possible, and to extend it for as long as possible. If unpleasant aspects of reality intrude, it will be with the loving support of a parent doing their best to empower and protect their child.

In this way, you facilitate the development of a sense of empowerment and control (self-esteem and confidence) into your child's basic self-object model. Later, when other competing messages are received that they are not powerful, or are defective, or not good enough, or should be ashamed to be alive, or should do something that does not feel right because someone claims authority over them or "knows better", they will have the power to resist. If not externally, at least internally; this will allow the possibility to rectify the situation later when external circumstances change.

The pediatrician and psychoanalyst Donald Winnecot coined the phrase "good enough mother", which has been widely misinterpreted, but in fact describes a mother (or other caretaker) who is able to provide just such an illusion of omnipotence for her infant child, which in turn allows a child's "true self" to take form.

If this were all that the method accomplished - the empowerment of our children - it would offer the possibility of transforming society and the world around us, as each generation passed on lesser and lesser levels of anxiety and fear, and greater and greater levels of contentment and happiness.

However, there is more. There is a wonderful synergy I have discovered, which offers the opportunity to recognize and overcome the self-limiting programming that pretty much all of us have unknowingly incorporated into our personal self-object models. Programming that limits our perceptions and understanding of the world, and keeps us from realizing what we are: Beings of immense power, understanding, and compassion.

A Perspective on Spirituality

"I am a man of fixed and unbending principles, the first of which is to be flexible at all times."
- Senator Everett Dirksen

Since one of the goals of Transformative Parenting™ is your transformation, as a parent, into a more empathic, empowered, and aware human being, let me spend some time talking about transformation in general. How and why it occurs, and methods of accomplishing it.

Transformation

Transformation implies change, generally lots of change. The first thing to note here is that personal change generally causes discomfort. In our discussion of objectification, we showed that anger and anxiety arise from conflicts in inner object models. Since our current behaviors and emotions are determined by our current object models (beliefs), saying that we want to change some of our behaviors or emotional responses implies we want to change the object models which are causing them.

Because of rigidity and identification, attempts to change previously created object models, particularly self-object models, is resisted; and the major manifestations of that resistance are anxiety, fear, and anger: In other words, psychic discomfort and even psychic pain.

The next thing to note is that it is normal to avoid pain. So if we are making a logical decision to consciously change ourselves, we must have some reason, some motivation, or foresee a goal or benefit (such as greater happiness, wisdom, knowledge, or self-confidence) which will offset the near-term psychological cost of enduring the discomfort required to create change.

That is, the pain of staying the same must be greater than the pain of change.

So undertaking a path of personal transformation is not to be taken lightly. It is hard work, but we anticipate big payoffs in the end.

Transformative Parenting™ is not easy. This is because parenting, at least good parenting, is never easy; and because transformation and self-change aren't easy either. We begin with a goal or goals in mind, which provide motivation and direction. We learn to recognize when something is wrong, identify what it is; and then we do the work to change it. It is not as simple as reading a book, but it can begin there.

As I see it, transformation requires the following things:

Recognizing the cost of staying the same
Motivation, seeing a payoff for making the change
Identifying what needs to change
Understanding how to make the change
Willingness to tolerate the discomfort.
Stubbornness to do it over and over.

For some people, recognizing a need to change is easy. If you are chronically miserable, anxious, depressed, fearful, or unhappy, it may be obvious to you that internal changes are necessary; both for your sake and your future, and also to prevent passing on these issues to your child. For others, the concerns may be more subtle: We recognize we are not as compassionate, understanding, or empowered as we would like to be. We recognize there are ways we are limiting ourselves, and likely those around us. Some of them we know about, and some we do not. Perhaps we are simply unsure of ourselves, and want to do our best as parents to ensure our children have the best chance in life to be happy.

In any case, we would like to become aware of faulty beliefs that cause limitations and conflict. Many of these were learned in childhood, perhaps before our earliest memories, and at this point are a part of our reality. We take them for granted even though they may not be true. We would like to become aware of these beliefs, so they can be re-examined. We want to determine if they are in fact still valid, or useless vestigial mental objects that are at best a waste of mental resources, and at worst hold us back in our spiritual, mental, physical, and social development, or keep us from being the kind of parent we want to be for our child.

Finally, we do not want to pass on these limitations to our children, who we would like to see grow into empowered, confident adults; in fact, even more empowered and confident than ourselves.

There are many systems of personal transformation. Some offer change in a particular direction: Stop drinking, stop smoking, be a better public speaker, make more money. Some offer employment or education: Becoming a lawyer, teacher, doctor, actor, carpenter, priest, etc. Some, like Transformative Parenting™, offer freedom from inner chains: Meditation, yoga, mysticism, saintly devotion and prayer, psychotherapy.

Often, we know some of our inner chains: Social anxiety, insecurity, mood swings, obsessions, compulsions, fears. However, many times the chains are invisible. We do not even know they are there, but something keeps us from trying to change our life circumstance, something keeps us from being happy.

Transformative Parenting™ offers a path to becoming a wonderful parent and in addition a path to personal freedom. It appeals to my proclivity towards efficiency. You get to "kill two birds with one stone". (As a vegetarian, I dislike that phrase, but it gets the point across perfectly.)

Some systems of transformation purport to be undertaken individually, and some require a guide. In my experience, where there is a competent guide available, they can be extremely helpful. Not only because the guide has experience and knowledge they can share with you in a tailored fashion, but also because the guide is not you. There is something about having a second set of eyes looking at a situation, which gives it more perspective - stereo vision as it were. This often allows the identification of issues that are invisible to you from your vantage point.

I have had many years of training in meditation, martial arts, psychotherapy, psychoanalysis, psychiatry, medicine, and miscellaneous life experience, all of which exposed personal issues and inner conflicts. Through all these endeavors, others made many of the most significant discoveries about me.

When these discoveries were pointed out, it was often painful, since many of these inner conflicts were hidden under layers of shame, anger, and guilt. However, with help and encouragement, I have been able to understand and accept myself more, and as a result also understand and accept others. At this point, one of my greatest satisfactions is helping people understand and accept themselves.

My life experience has taken me where I am, just as yours has taken you where you are. We all have a unique Way or path to follow, because our life experience and genetic inheritance are different. In kung fu training, this is expressed by saying, "My kung fu is my kung fu, and your kung fu is your kung fu." It comes across as haughty, when told by a senior student or teacher to a newcomer, but it is a simple fact. Accepting it can go a long way to helping us find happiness.

So, what can I recommend to those, especially parents, who wish to pursue a path of personal transformation?

Up until now, those who wanted to pursue a path of freedom (some say "enlightenment" or "actualization", I sometimes say "awareness") have had to make difficult life choices. Many of these paths are quite arduous, and it is difficult to pursue them while raising a family, because of time, distance, and money. If only we were fortunate enough to have an Enlightened Master with us all the time; someone who could point out to us when we had gone astray, and give us a shove in the right direction. This is one of the great benefits of those who live in ashrams and monasteries, and why so many of the celebrated spiritual masters graduated from that environment.

However, I have made a wonderful discovery. That as a parent, you do have available a most effective spiritual guide. Someone who is always there, and who can almost effortlessly point out to you the invisible chains that bind you. Once the chains are pointed out, you can then choose to remove them.

That wonderful being, your guide in the spiritual path of Transformative Parenting™, is your child.

Enlightenment

> *"When in the conclave they elected me pope, I asked for some time alone before I accepted," he said in the interview. "I was overwhelmed by great anxiety, then I closed my eyes and all thoughts, including the possibility of refusing, went away."*
> *- Pope Francis*

Since my youth, I have been fascinated by the idea of enlightenment: What it is, and how to obtain it. To have had a book like this back then would have been wonderful. However, I am aware that for many people the word itself is off-putting, rather than an attraction. Therefore, I would like to talk a bit about enlightenment, define it, explain why it is helpful to make an effort to experience it, and how it relates to Transformative Parenting™.

Here is my definition, with the caveat as I mentioned at the beginning of the book, that words are only imprecise pointers.

Enlightenment is a state of the alert mind where objectification (or thinking), is interrupted or suspended. What remains is a state of awareness, characterized by a lack of interpretation, judgment, or thought.

Presence, present-moment awareness, non-ego state, peak state, being in the now, and other words and phrases have also been used as conceptual pointers to this non-conceptual experience.

Presence does not necessarily endow special powers. However, since in this state you perceive without the clouding overlay of preexisting inner models, as you slip back into ordinary consciousness you may perceive novel and perhaps very subtle characteristics of external objects, which were previously unnoticed. We might call this *insight.* This is one reason the cultivation of enlightenment is useful from our standpoint. We are able to re-evaluate whatever circumstance we are in in new ways, often on a more basic and meaningful level than our usual, highly abstracted and conflicted, conscious state will allow.

Enlightenment is generally experienced in brief moments of time, though if you are gifted or practiced the periods can be longer. However, even highly enlightened people must spend a great deal of time in ordinary consciousness, unless they have others caring for them. Hence, they continue to be exposed to and interact with their inner object models. This is necessary to function in the world: to find food, shelter, make money, etc.

Repeatedly going to this primal, simple state of mind tends to induce simplification in ordinary thinking, feeling, and behavior. Not that you can't think about abstract or complex things when necessary, but more that you are drawn to simplicity and efficiency, in thought, form, and action.

You are also less likely to be distracted from important issues when they arise. In other words, your priorities are clearer.

As Buddha first described, the practice of enlightenment allows the direct insight that pain and suffering is created by attachment to inner object models, and particularly from attachment to inner self-object models (beliefs about "me"). With this insight you become less affected by whatever pain and suffering you are experiencing. On the other hand, depending on the path you follow, you may well become more aware of the pain and suffering of others.

Thus, by working towards enlightenment you become more compassionate, aware, and effective in life.

There are many ways of encouraging a non-ego state of awareness (ego being another word for "I" or "me"); for example, some forms of meditation, and physical arts. There are also paths of devotion, which lie at the core of Judaism, Christianity, Islam, Hinduism, and most other religions. Choose the path that is most suitable for you, your interests, and your circumstances.

Transformative Parenting™, besides being an optimal parenting methodology, is also a path towards enlightenment. As you continue in its practice, you will experience these benefits yourself, while at the same time raising a magnificent child.

The Gift of Death

Though worthwhile to attempt, enlightenment, or freedom from conceptualization or objectification is very difficult to attain. The mind in its aspect of objectifier (object model creator, manipulator and referencer) is arguably the most powerful, generally the most pervasive part of our conscious being. Attempting to shut down objectification, even considering the possibility, will usually induce a frightened, self-protective reaction that causes us to "think" even more intently. This is because the objectifying aspect of our minds is precisely what we identify with most strongly. René Descartes' words: "I think, therefore I am.", are felt true because "I" is for most of us precisely that part of ourselves which thinks, and thinking is an aspect of objectification. When faced with the prospect of not thinking, we are, in effect, facing oblivion and death; quite terrifying for most of us.

As I said, this aspect of our minds is extremely powerful, self-protective, and used to being "the boss". Because of that, enlightenment is not possible unless the mind itself is enlisted to help.

I would like your mind to understand and accept that it is helpful to stop constantly objectifying everything around you, at least for short periods. There are benefits to doing so, and if you stop thinking for a while, it does not mean you will never think again or you will no longer be "you". Please try to trust that is so. The "you" that results from the experience will be enriched, and thus greater than the "you" that came before.

A request for trust from me is all well and good of course, but a healthy, powerful mind will require proof that it is not Lord of the Universe, and likely yours is healthy and powerful. This is the reason Zen koans were developed, and why there are so many scholarly works devoted to elucidating and refining the understanding of what is essentially a quest to quiet the mind, which from the outside would seem so simple, until you try it yourself.

No, unless the mind is shown clearly the fact of its limitation, that it is not all-powerful, it will not let go of what it does so well - sustaining your personal universe. This is a survival instinct, both for the mind as an abstract entity, and for the body, which relies on the mind for its physical survival.

Pondering this dilemma though, and observing everyday life, we find a solution: The evident reality that we do not survive. The inevitability of our death, and more importantly our acceptance of it, can be our salvation.

Death is not something the mind accepts easily, especially its own death. Most of us spend most of our lives avoiding thinking about it, and it is precisely for the reason above.

"Me" not existing, is not acceptable. We choose, or rather, our minds choose, not to consider our finiteness, despite the evidence; because it would force our mind to realize it has limits, and is powerless in the face of death.

There are many who will strongly object to this, and the amount of effort people put into trying to become immortal or stay young forever is immense. I have heard at various times, that if only we could live in harmony with the world, or we could appropriately regulate our chi energy, or take the right herbs at the right times, it would be possible to live forever. In response, I ask for the evidence: Is there even one person who has done it? One would think that if it were indeed possible, at least one person out of all the billions of people who have lived would have lived at least a long, long time. We would be able to go visit them and ask how they did it. However, as far as I have seen, the maximum life span seems to be around 120 years. Most of us will live for much less time than that. Even in biblical accounts, almost everyone dies eventually.

Having lived a few generations now, I have watched as in each generation a wave of young people take a great stand for immortality. They state that aging and death are a result of this or that, and not inevitable. Of course, who wouldn't want to believe them, and I'm not saying they don't believe it themselves. However, it is clear they are wrong.

On reflection, and after much study and research, it seems that in fact nothing lasts forever. Even stars die eventually.

If one can face this fact directly, and accept it, all sorts of unexpected benefits accrue. One benefit is that the mind becomes more willing to "go there". Something about inevitability makes things less fearsome. Inevitable things are more easily accepted. The mind on some level realizes that attaching an emotional feeling to an inevitable occurrence is a waste of energy. If something is not inevitable, attaching an emotional component to it will provide a motivation to the organism (person, mind); either to struggle to avoid the thing if it is unpleasant, or to obtain the thing if it is pleasant. If something is inevitable, there is no need for motivation, one way or the other, and hence no need for emotionality about it.

In the case of death, fear about it is reduced if its inevitability is accepted.

Another benefit of accepting inevitable death is that you can see more clearly whether your actions, in a finite life, make sense. The inner object model of life is corrected, and a reorientation of priorities takes place. Does it really matter if I become a millionaire? If I get that yacht, or a second or third home? If I can squeeze an extra 20% out of this desperate seller, or pay my assistant or housekeeper less? Get an extra point out of that bond issuer? Does it matter if other people think I'm cool? If I have the latest fashions?

Often, you realize that most of what you felt was important, really is not important at all. Then, as did Viktor Frankl, you begin a search for true meaning: In the face of death, what really does matter?

Many people who choose or are forced to accept death, begin to view life differently: more as a precious gift than as a burden or a right. From that view arises gratitude. Combine gratitude with compassion, and there arises a desire to help others have happier lives.

With the compassion that arises from understanding we are all acting in strict accordance with our unique life conditioning and circumstance, we realize that changing the lives of the less fortunate involves changing their circumstances, which is the only way to alter conditioning. Those of us with money, power, empathy, or knowledge, can attempt to change the circumstances of the less fortunate by using the resources we have been blessed with.

Moreover, beyond our lifetimes, we begin to wish to ensure that future generations can also enjoy the gift of a happy and fulfilling life.

For parents and caregivers of children, this can be very reaffirming, or cause for drastic life changes, depending on your previous orientation. To put it another way, parenting, in contrast to many other endeavors, does have enduring meaning: not simply because of its lasting impact on humanity, but also in the journey. Because parenting is best understood as a journey, with each moment (painful or joyous) savored and treasured without regard for future outcomes or rewards.

It has been my experience that parents at the end of their lives, who have given their all in love, time, and commitment to their children, find happiness and contentment, even if they die poor. You can't take money with you. Love, on the other hand, may be a different story.

Discipleship

In addition to triggering the fear of oblivion or death, reaching the state of mind we are calling enlightenment is tricky because there is no inner object to which we can orient ourselves in thinking about it. The seeking of an inner object (a word, idea or memory) to describe the state, is directly counter to being in the state we are looking for. Therefore, words and thoughts cannot get us to enlightenment. We can only get ourselves in the general vicinity of where we are trying to be, then "let go", and hope we drift into the mental state we are seeking. There is a bit of luck involved, and for most, many attempts.

In traditional methods of enlightenment training, there are individual mental practices that train the mind to stay focused on one thing. After doing that for a while, one attempts to focus on "nothing", or perhaps "everything". This gets you in the general neighborhood of enlightenment. It is not quite right, but it's close.

To get to the exact location, there is another great help: Being in close proximity to an enlightened person. As one associates closely with anyone, given a receptive state of mind, through various mechanisms something of their state of mind is transferred to you. This process can be enhanced by consciously attuning to them, and then maintaining that attunement (which by the way helps train focus and attention as well).

For this reason, it can be a great blessing to attend to the needs of an enlightened master. To the outsider, it may seem as though the student is worshiping the guru or master (which can happen), or as though the master is manipulating or exploiting the student. Not to say that exploitation doesn't happen, because I'm sure there are many who pretend to be masters who are not, but the inside story is more symbiotic.

In a true guru-disciple relationship both are benefiting; the acolyte more than the guru. By being in close proximity with the teacher, the student absorbs the qualities of the teacher, learns directly, wordlessly, what it is to be enlightened, and can stay in tune with the master as he or she goes into an enlightened state. This is what some call *transmission.*

As part of my preparation to be a parent, I spent a number of years studying Chinese kung fu under the tutelage of my sifu (teacher), and my sigung (teacher's teacher). Decorum and manners are an important part of kung fu training, and one aspect of that is how the student carries him or herself while with the teacher, and away from the quan or training area.

Once, as I was making ready to accompany Sigung on a trip to China, Sifu instructed me on how I should take care of him. Essentially, my job was to protect him, not just physically, but also mentally. Sifu described creating and maintaining a calm, protective "bubble", centered around Sigung, as I went with him about his daily affairs.

To do this, a disciple must maintain constant awareness of the periphery, the space inside the bubble, and the teacher's state of mind. Ideally, if some danger arises outside the periphery, one can maneuver the teacher around the danger without the teacher ever being aware of the situation in the first place, or at least having the trouble extend into the area of the protective bubble. Conversely, as one is attuned to the teacher's state, one can become aware of the teacher's needs and see that they are met, either by moving the bubble, or changing the environment; sometimes without the need being stated or even conscious in the teacher at all. In any case, a sense of calm should be maintained within the protective bubble surrounding the teacher at all times.

By following this process, the disciple learns how to maintain simultaneous awareness of the inner state of the teacher, and the external environment, and how to mediate the two in a harmonious manner. Though a difficult and draining process, this practice is the transformative advantage of taking trips away from the home environment, made more difficult by the occasional capricious actions of your teacher!

If you watch carefully, you can observe similar behavior in many other situations in life: The Secret Service protecting the President, the Armed Forces protecting the Nation, an honorable police officer protecting civilians, a father protecting his family, a mother protecting her child.

This exercise can be adapted in many ways. In a later chapter, I will explain how we use it in Transformative Parenting.

Learning From Your Child

"(1) At the same time came the disciples unto Jesus, saying, Who is the greatest in the kingdom of heaven? (2) And Jesus called a little child unto him, and set him in the midst of them, (3) And said, Verily I say unto you, Except ye be converted, and become as little children, ye shall not enter into the kingdom of heaven. (4) Whosoever therefore shall humble himself as this little child, the same is greatest in the kingdom of heaven. (5) And whoso shall receive one such little child in my name receiveth me. (6) But whoso shall offend one of these little ones which believe in me, it were better for him that a millstone were hanged about his neck, and that he were drowned in the depth of the sea.
(10) Take heed that ye despise not one of these little ones; for I say unto you, That in heaven their angels do always behold the face of my Father which is in heaven."
- Jesus

A child is a special human being, and not because of their neediness or "cuteness". Children are special because they are in or closer to a state of enlightenment.

In the earliest months, children operate almost entirely without inner object models. They perceive things directly, without preconditioned knowledge, ideas, hypotheses, or value judgments. Later, forms and patterns are assimilated into defined internal models, but initially almost all experiences are fresh and new.

There is a joy of living in healthy children that is infectious and irresistible to adults; unless they are so repressed they cannot allow themselves to harmonize with it.

Adults are filled with knowledge, in fact, overwhelmed with knowledge and thinking to the point it dictates our lives and emotions. Children on the other hand, are empty of knowledge, or have only rudimentary knowledge, and so are generally filled with optimism, and aware only of boundless possibility (at least when they are protected from fears of being helpless, misunderstood, or alone).

To put it another way, there is a divine spark in children, which in most adults has been quenched or turned to a smoldering ember. The possibility exists, however, to re-kindle our spark, and fan and support our children's spark, and turn them both into powerful flames.

Wouldn't it be wonderful if we could be open and optimistic, filled with the joy of living, able to experience every moment of our short lives fully? Well, we can, but only if we allow our children to teach us how. This is the crux of Transformative Parenting™: The recognition that both child and adult bring something very valuable to the table. A parent brings the technical knowledge and emotional sensitivity necessary for survival, and their child shows them how to live in freedom, joy, and spontaneity. Not only does a parent teach their child, a child teaches their parent.

> *"The soul is healed by being with children."*
> *- Fyodor Dostoevsky*

For this two-way learning to occur, respect and admiration must flow in both directions. Respect and admiration for adults are automatic in children, unless they have been hurt or abused. Respect and admiration, even reverence for children, should also be present in adults or we will not be able to learn from them.

Children are co-creators of their own universe, just as all humans, indeed all sentient beings, are. It is our awesome responsibility as parents to help shape that universe. A child has gifts to offer us as well. If we are willing to accept those gifts, we can reshape our own personal universe into one more filled with potential and opportunity, and less restricted by psychological limitations. We can come closer to "heaven on earth".

For those who have had rigid upbringings, such as members of fundamentalist religious groups, or other rigid cultural or family backgrounds, the idea that a child has any sort of "wisdom" to impart to an adult will generate either an intense negative emotional response (anger), or a cold dismissal (depending on their learned relationship to internal emotion). This is expected. Your inner object model of parenting, shaped by your own experience of being parented and reinforced by your culture, is threatened. As a result, because of identification with that model you are feeling threatened. It is a mirage. I am not threatening you. I am asking you to reconsider that aspect of your model of parenting, and that aspect of yourself that does not feel empowered to change your model of parenting, or yourself. Take a breath, reflect, and keep reading.

In conflicts with others, and particularly our children, we can make the most important discoveries about ourselves (and our cultures, inasmuch as they are integrated into our self-object model).

Transforming Anger

In order to recognize those discoveries and learn from them, it is critical for you to maintain an awareness of your emotional state, and recognize particularly two "red flag" emotional states: Anger and dismissal. The combination seems to me very close to "despise" as in Jesus' quote above.

Whenever you note the presence of these emotions in relation to a child, there is something wrong: not with your child, but with you. Take a step back and figure out what it is. You have an inner object model of your child, yourself, or the environment, which is incorrect and needs to be changed.

Rather than fluidly altering the model, because of its rigidity and your identification with it, a negative emotional response has been generated and directed at your child, who is perceived as threatening your model, and thus you. It is a mirage. Your child is not threatening your existence. He or she has helped you find a flaw in one of your inner object models.

Take a breath. Can you identify the model that is incorrect, the change that needs to be made (in you, or the environment)? If not, it may require later reflection. In any event, drop the anger or disdain, apologize to your child if you have hurt them (physically or mentally), resolve the situation calmly (but not coldly), and keep parenting. You are now parenting in a way that will lead to transformation; you are practicing Transformative Parenting™.

If you learn nothing else from this book but the practice of re-interpreting anger, it will be more than enough. Both you and your child will happier, your lives will be enriched with wisdom and understanding, and the world will become a better place through your example.

> *"For every minute you are angry you lose sixty seconds of happiness."*
> *- Ralph Waldo Emerson*

"No"

"Whatever words we utter should be chosen with care, for people will hear them and be influenced by them, for good or ill."
- Buddha

When I was training to be a psychoanalyst, one of the other candidates confided to me that she had trouble saying "No" to her daughter. In her mind, she visualized her child as a growing tree, and every time she said "No", she was pruning a budding branch.

This comparison of a child to a growing tree I find quite profound, and I have heard bonsai masters make the same analogy. Pruning a tree can be helpful in shaping it to its environment. On the other hand, excessive pruning will damage and stunt the tree's growth. In the same way, correction of children is sometimes necessary and helpful, if done carefully and kept to a minimum. Too much correction, and correction done harshly, is damaging to a child; just as excessive pruning, or pruning done incorrectly is damaging to a tree.

In the past, social mobility was severely restricted. Change was slower. Perhaps a larger degree of "pruning" for a child made sense. However, in today's world change is constant. Children frequently move into different social classes and geographic areas other than those of their parents. In contrast to a tree, where its environment is mostly fixed and stable, a child must be prepared for change. Excessive correction in childhood limits the later adult's flexibility and adaptability, and hence their ability to survive and thrive.

Children should be honored, and treated with reverence and respect. If a child does something that you consider a mistake, the situation must be assessed carefully. Is this really a mistake, or is your child teaching you something about themselves, the world, or you, that was previously misinterpreted, unnoticed or discarded?

Not only that, but we need to remember that mistakes are expected. We all make mistakes. In fact, learning is impossible without making mistakes. So a child making a mistake should not be greeted with anger, because anger will discourage curiosity. Encourage the seeking that led to the mistake, even if you feel you must draw attention to the mistake. Your emotional response should be weighed carefully to assure that the zone of security, which you have established around your child, remains calm.

> *"I have failed over and over again - that is why I succeed."*
> *- Michael Jordan*

A child is naturally curious and exploring. Discovery often involves breaking things, and making what appears to the parent to be a mess. The urge to say "No" must be controlled if your child's natural curiosity and acquisition of knowledge are to be encouraged, and for you to undo those parts of your past conditioning which are best discarded. The reality your child is experiencing is different from the reality you grew up in. Your reality has also changed. Let your child show you how it differs, and be willing to let them teach you. The impulse to say "No" is a signal that your opportunity for learning may be at hand.

Another issue with "No" is that it is too broad, and too loaded with emotional power. When you suddenly yell "NO!" at a child, you will observe them freeze, and an anguished look, or numb expression appear on their face. This is because they do not realize exactly what they are doing wrong, so they stop everything. They may also anticipate violence. Although you might later explain specifically what you had an issue with, in that moment you have laid down a negative association to potentially anything they were doing or attempting to do.

For example, your child is drawing with crayons, or playing with fingerpaints. They begin to stray outside the paper, and draw or paint on the floor. You go out of the room for a moment, and come back to see the mess on the floor. You react with an angry "NO!" Note that your child is initially at a loss as to what they have done wrong. For all they know, you don't like the color they've chosen, the paper they have used, or perhaps you don't want them to draw at all. Even if you explain later, the negative association has been imprinted on whatever they guessed was the problem in that moment. These faulty associations can be hard to undo later on, say when you would like to encourage your child's artistic ability, or creativity.

It is rare that a child must be abruptly controlled; perhaps if they are threatened with sudden danger by running out into a busy street, or they are about to stick an object into a power outlet. However, note the fault of the caregiver for not paying close enough attention to their child or the surroundings. Their child is only doing what is natural for them to do, which is to explore and test their environment. You need not react in anger. Just remove the danger and explain why you are not allowing that particular behavior. If you find it hard to explain, it may be the activity is not as dangerous as you thought!

If your child runs into the street, get them quickly and calmly, bring them back to the sidewalk, explain that the street is dangerous, and why, and how it makes mommy or daddy afraid when they go into the street without you.

If your child tries to put something into a power outlet, gently move them away. Explain that it is dangerous to put things in the power outlets, that doing so can hurt them a lot, and it scares mommy or daddy when they do so. Then observe them to make sure they understood what you told them and are ready to accept it. Search for a least-restrictive way of assuring their safety.

These actions may need to be repeated many times, which does not mean your child is "bad", "defiant", or "oppositional". They are being normal: exploring and testing the world around them, developing their senses, physical skills and object models, and learning how to use them.

Sometimes fear for their child triggers a parent's angry outburst. However, anger sends the message to a child that they are "bad". It is better to simply honor and accept your original emotion of fear than to let it become anger. If you inadvertently express your fear as anger, be willing to apologize to your child promptly when you realize your mistake.

If a child is consistently treated or referred to as "bad", "defiant", or "oppositional", they will likely become so, unless the abuse is so severe that their spirit is crushed. In that case, you and your child will likely carry that "millstone" (of shame and grief) around your necks for the rest of your lives (and perhaps beyond, if Jesus was correct).

I once heard the story of a Buddhist master who was on a very long journey. Part of his retinue was a most irascible personal cook who was extremely rude and difficult with everyone. Despite this, the master never displayed any sign of being upset about his behavior. When asked why he put up with the man, the master replied: "He is not only my cook; he also teaches me patience". This is a powerful spiritual practice: Look upon those who anger you as your teacher. They are teaching you by activating the self-object models that make you angry, which gives you an opportunity to re-examine those models in light of new knowledge and understanding.

I define patience is the ability to sit quietly with discomfort. In our model, discomfort or anxiety arises due to a mismatch or conflict between two or more of our inner object models. Possibly, an expectation or hope for our future that has remained unmet.

Remind yourself that life is in the journey and not the final result, which is inevitable anyway. Let your child teach you patience, and about yourself. In doing so, you also teach them patience. You each only have this opportunity, this moment, once. Make the most of it.

Knowledge, Learning, Teaching

"..in order to seek truth, it is necessary once in the course of our life, to doubt, as far as possible, of all things."
- René Descartes

When I was in medical school, our Dean used to tell us that in order to have gotten where we were, we had to have demonstrated a thirst for knowledge. Unfortunately, we now found ourselves tied to a fire hydrant of knowledge, with the spigot opened wide.

In medical school, there is a vast amount of information to assimilate. It is not possible to learn or retain it all, and the struggle to do so is quite uncomfortable, especially for someone who aspired to be a general practitioner in a rural area, and so needed to know it all.

I also remember a lecture where another professor apologetically told us that studies had been done which looked back at the evolution of medical knowledge over time. The studies showed that historically, up to half of what doctors learned would later turn out to be misleading, insufficient, or wrong. However, there was no way to tell the good from the bad ahead of time, and so our instructors had to teach us all they knew or thought they knew.

While medical knowledge is a particular example, I believe the general knowledge we have acquired over our lifetimes has these same problems: There is too much of it, we know a lot of it is incorrect, and it is impossible to separate what is correct from what is not.

We learn most of what we know from others: parents, other family, neighbors and friends, radio, podcasts, books, magazines, the internet, television, and movies. Moreover, those who passed this information on to us generally got their information in the same way: by listening to, or watching others.

If you look, you can find books by experts in their fields (not to mention people who pretend to be experts) which disagree entirely with one another. Forget about trusting magazines, television, or the Internet, because most of those outlets are tripping over each other to publish the most outlandish and potentially trumped-up things, out of a desire to boost ratings and thereby increase advertising sales.

Even seemingly trustworthy learning is suspect, for at least three reasons: First, there is no way of determining if the original source of the knowledge really knew what they were talking about. Second, even if they did, that information was likely altered substantially by the time it reached your eyes or ears. And third, that knowledge may have only been valid for a particular circumstance and time.

An experiment used in studies of eyewitness reliability in criminal studies, and psychology classes, is to stage a sudden unexpected event, done by a stranger or a few people who afterwards leave quickly. Each person in the class is asked to write down exactly what they saw (colors, details, descriptions), and the accounts are compared. It is remarkable how widely people's memories of the same event differ from each other, and from what actually occurred.

This experiment teaches us how unreliable information can be even when reported "first-hand" from someone who was actually there.

Many of us have at one time or another played the game "Whisper Down the Lane", where someone makes up a short story, then whispers it in the ear of the person next to them. That person then whispers it into the ear of another person, and so on. Usually after only a few people, the story has shifted in very significant ways.

This game is actually a very important experiment for each of us to perform. It shows how fragile verbal communication is as a method of passing on reliable knowledge. In American jurisprudence, information obtained this way is considered so unreliable it is disallowed as "hearsay".

Very often, knowledge can be valid for particular people at particular times, but is not valid for others or at other times.

For example, people's perceptions of law enforcement officers are shaped dramatically by where they have grown up. In some areas, police are regarded primarily as helpful, even heroic defenders of public safety. In other places, they are regarded as untrustworthy, intrusive bullies. People in both camps may be able to back up their opinion with repeated personal experience, and so both groups are "right" in their opinions, given their particular circumstances. However, they would both be "wrong" and perhaps even in danger if they found themselves in the other group's environment for some reason.

Here are some quotes from famous dictators, which illustrate that knowledge which is relatively valid for a particular person at a particular time can be inappropriate or wrong for others:

> *"When there's a person, there's a problem. When there's no person, there's no problem."*
> *- Joseph Stalin*

> *"Make the lie big, make it simple, keep saying it, and eventually they will believe it.*
> *- Adolph Hitler*

With incorrect knowledge, even a little in the wrong places can cause severe social and intellectual dysfunction. If the possessor has power over others, incorrect knowledge can cause real hardship to the people he or she controls.

> *"Beware of false knowledge; it is more dangerous than ignorance."*
> *- George Bernard Shaw*

In the framework we are using here, incorrect knowledge equates to incorrect object models, and incorrect object models are more prone to produce conflicts with reality than "more correct" ones.

You should always question the validity of what you hear and read. Does it fit with what you already know to be true? On the other hand, could this be new, valid information, which is going to cause you to have to re-evaluate previously long-held beliefs? Strive to be open to both possibilities.

Is there any way to know what is true? In the sense of "The Truth", I doubt it. The first words of the Tao Te Ching: "The Tao which can be spoken is not the true Tao." are instructive. Whenever we try to frame truth in terms of words, we can only offer an approximation at best.

> *"The water in a vessel is sparkling; the water in the sea is dark. The small truth has words which are clear; the great truth has great silence."*
> *- Rabindranath Tagore*

The "small truth" which Tagore is talking about corresponds to the "relative truth" or relatively valid truth we discussed in the first section of the book. Almost all of what we "know" fits within this category.

I once attended a spiritual retreat where one of the exercises involved activating and visualizing the chakras (energy centers in some Eastern models of physiology). We were later paired with an experienced teacher for help and advice. I confided to my mentor my concern that I did not perceive the chakras in the colors I was supposed to. He told me something that seemed scandalous at the time, but I am now grateful for. To paraphrase: Don't blindly accept as true anything you haven't experienced for yourself. And I would add: preferably through multiple experiences in various circumstances.

Unfortunately, with the world as complex as it is, we are forced to learn from trusted authority. There is simply not enough time to learn everything from experience.

However, it is a good idea to remain open to changing your mind about anything you have not directly observed. Moreover, if you have direct knowledge of something which conflicts with trusted authority, your direct experience should be given more weight.

Let the world be your final arbiter, and not any particular book or human being. No book is perfect, even one which honestly attempts to reflect reality, because it is only made of words, which as we have seen are imperfect pointers to meaning, and because it can at best only reflect its author's relative view of reality. In addition, no human being is perfect, unless we apply the fallacy of idealization.

This is the essence of the scientific method, and while I struggle with the fact that scientific evidence is sometimes obtained in immoral and inhumane ways, its reliance on direct observation is its strength. Unfortunately, as with other media, scientific literature is bedeviled with studies that were faked, poorly designed, or poorly reported, and so must also be taken with a grain of salt, and weighed against your own direct experience.

In summary, the best approach to learning (and teaching) is to combine essential learning from authority with experiential verification. This is done in mathematics by doing homework problems, and in science classes by having labs, where hopefully experimental results confirm the validity of the theories being taught. In our life experience, we can strive to be objective and observant, while being open to re-evaluating previously held beliefs in light of whatever new experience or evidence the universe provides us.

The Method of No Method

When I was a serious student of kung fu, Sigung explained to me his method of teaching, which he called the "Method of No Method". The idea is that only the basic ideas of theory and practice are provided. The students then work together to explore possibilities. If one has an idea, they take it to the practice area, and working together test it. If the idea works, they progress, and the students around them progress as well. If it doesn't work, the idea is discarded. Only occasionally, will the teacher critique or give a suggestion, and even more rarely "touch hands" with the students.

As we sat at a dinner table one night, he used a saltshaker to represent a student, whose goal was to reach the end of the table, which represented mastery and freedom. The major problem for the student is that they cannot see the end of the table from their perspective. The student starts off in the right general direction, set by the basic teaching, but is given freedom to discover in his own way. The teacher intervenes only rarely, to keep the saltshaker from falling off the wrong side of the table, or to provide encouragement. In Sigung's way of seeing things, kung fu is a very personal thing. Each person's kung fu should be their own. If a teacher "touches hands" too much with a student, they will naturally copy the teacher's way of doing things, thinking it must be the right way. However, the goal of kung fu training is not to produce a clone of the teacher; it is to make you free, as an individual: a master in your own right, in your own way.

Sigung himself was hesitant about applying his method to child rearing; I believe because he came from a Chinese culture that has multiply layered social rules, which are strongly enforced. However, coming from a culture that ostensibly supports the freedom of the individual, I believe it is an excellent approach, and in any event likely captures how most important learning takes place anyway.

The Method of No Method, is not the "School of Hard Knocks". In the School of Hard Knocks, one learns solely from experience, slowly and painfully, without the benefit of a benevolent guide or mentor. This is the school that those who have no parents, or have only abusive or neglectful parents, must learn from. Unfortunately, the knowledge they learn is limited, and only valid for dealing with harsh, abusive situations. As a result, they do not know how to behave in polite society, and become misfits, and outcasts, or at best, grow up feeling like misfits. This result is often magnified by a difficulty with empathic connection, because empathy is hard to learn if it has never been shown.

In the Method of No-Method, there is basic guidance and theory, and the instructor (parent) is present to avert clear danger. The teacher is free to suggest areas of possible study, engage in supportive dialog, even show and explain a few things, but if things are going well, generally lets the student explore and discover with minimal interference.

The Method of No-Method can be useful in parenting when done properly. Parents of course need to spend time teaching their children such things as vocabulary, the alphabet, numbers, colors, and the myriad of other essential things that can and should be learned in the family environment. However, teaching can be done in a friendly, supportive, fun way, which encourages a child's natural curiosity. Curiosity is suppressed in traditional methods of forced learning, but if encouraged and handled properly, curiosity will impel a child to discover for themselves most of what they need to know in life.

> *"If you are a parent, open doors to unknown directions to the child so he can explore. Don't make him afraid of the unknown, give him support."*
> *- Osho*

Much knowledge is acquired and validated through interactions with other children, and that learning is very important to the development of a healthy individual. This social knowledge is of a higher level of validity than that learned by rote, or simply being told, because it is usually validated by repeated experience, and supported by multiple observers who are peers and therefore more trusted.

> *"Example isn't another way to teach, it is the only way to teach."*
> *- Albert Einstein*

We should also be aware that children learn vast amounts from simply observing and copying the actions of their parents. For better or worse, this is normal and must be accepted. This is why the adage: "Do as I say and not as I do.", causes such conflict within a child, and between a parent and their child. Parents need to do as they say, acknowledge when they fail, and not be surprised or harsh when their children copy their actions and not their words.

> *"Children have never been very good at listening to their elders, but they have never failed to imitate them."*
> *- James Baldwin*

Formal schooling represents a transition phase where most learning begins to occur outside the presence of a parent, though parents still need to be present when they can, and vigilant in monitoring the lessons their child is learning. Self-respect, and respect for others, should always be encouraged. Threats from bullying, or warning signs such as poor grades, or anxiety about going to school or extracurricular activities should be dealt with quickly and supportively.

In later childhood, particularly in adolescence, the struggle for independence and autonomy from parents intersects with increasing capability. At some point in the process, the constant presence and intrusion of the parent can be reduced to occasional advice and offers of support. This is where the Method of No Method is again very useful. Parents eventually need to let go and allow their children to become adults. If a child has the experience of being allowed their own way to some extent in childhood, they are able to acquire and test the inner object models necessary to be comfortably and safely independent when they are adults.

In Transformative Parenting™, we are constantly evaluating our inner object models in light of the information our children bring us, and the emotional responses we are having to them. If we (and they) are at peace, or pleasantly excited, and we are feeling in harmony with them, we are doing well. If not, there may well be object models we are using that need modification.

In addition, we constantly evaluate the information we are teaching, doing our best not to teach as fact what we do not know for sure to be fact. It is better to admit ignorance than to teach a falsehood: State an opinion as an opinion, and a belief as a belief, not a fact. This way you give children (and others) a firm foundation of valid, functional object models, which will be useful in a wide variety of circumstances throughout life.

> *Shall I teach you what is knowledge? When you know a thing, say that you know it; when you do not know a thing, admit that you do not know it. That is knowledge."*
> *- Confucius*

Praise

Do not get so hung up in "truth" that you forget the importance of positive opinion statements. Don't be stingy with statements like: "I think you're really beautiful" or "handsome", or "smart", or "talented".

However, avoid "smarter than", or "prettier than", or comparisons to other people. Positive comparison statements may create momentary feelings of pleasure (mainly because your child feels your happiness in saying them), but they create long-term feelings of insecurity for both of you, and also teach pleasure at the expense of someone else's pain.

Finally, avoid criticizing a child, period. Either outright, as in: "You're stupid", or by comparison; "Why can't you be good like your brother?" This simply erodes their sense of self-worth, sabotaging whatever chance they might have of feeling confident and secure.

Attachment and Duty

"Whatever you are, be a good one."
- Abraham Lincoln

Transformative Parenting™ has the twin goals of raising an optimally functioning, empathic, independently-minded child; and bringing the parent, over time, to a freer, more aware state of consciousness, which combines the best qualities of adulthood and childhood.

Despite that, I do not believe the attainment of enlightenment is a desirable primary goal for parents. At least not until your children are grown and fully independent adults. Full enlightenment corresponds to the ability to stay in the enlightened state for an extended period, and the proclivity to do so. Unfortunately, in order for that to occur you will have broken or weakened most of the bonds of attachment to material forms, which would necessarily include your child.

In Transformative Parenting™, we use our attachment as a motivator and guide during the phase of parenting in which we have physical contact with our children. In a kind of judo move, our attachment to our child frees us from attachment to other physical forms, and indirectly propels us on the path of enlightenment.

For the benefit of my enlightened readers, I mention briefly the possibility of *duty* as might be applied to parenting by an enlightened being. Sometimes, a person undertakes a task because it is their duty to do so, because of their unique karma or situation or role in life. The universe needs them to do the task, and so they do it in accordance with the desire or promptings of the universe. An enlightened being is happy doing what the universe requires of them, and to the best of their ability. They may even enjoy doing the task, but the trick here is that they would equally enjoy whatever reasonable task was necessary. They are not "attached" to the particular task that the universe has assigned them, and would be fine doing another.

Therefore, an enlightened person could become a parent, or run an orphanage or school, and do a wonderful job. They would be attentive, sensitive, caring, even loving. The children or students would feel loved and cherished. Another positive, is that the enlightened person would not be "clingy", and would love them for themselves, and not because they could do particular things for them, and when the time came, could let them go without anguish or pain.

For parents, I do not think it is worthwhile to strive too hard to achieve this state. If it happens, fine - no one will be the worse for it. However, if you get caught up in expectations one way or the other, it will really muck things up. If you strive too hard, you will neglect your child and your duty. If you try hard, and fail, you will undermine your sense of self-worth and perhaps that of your child.

Embrace the fact that nature has made you attached to your child, and your child attached to you. It will make everything easier for you except the final stage: when you let your child go into the world as an adult. Then, you may well feel a great pain of loss because of your attachment.

Know there is a cost to everything, and this is the appropriate time to pay the price for the joy and wisdom raising your child has brought you. Also know that acceptance of this pain brings the opportunity for further spiritual growth.

(Be careful though, sometimes attachment can get out of hand, and need to be controlled. There exists a needy, poisonous form of attachment, felt by the parent to be love, which is controlling, engulfing, and smothering - out of touch with the needs and desires of their child.)

I recommend you use the attachment and love you feel towards your child to keep you motivated towards the goal: raising a self-confident, independent, emotionally secure person. In fact, I think it is very helpful if you can make a conscious decision that this is your primary goal in life.

Even if your primary goal in life has been something else (i.e. become enlightened, or famous, make lots of money) - acknowledge that you are a parent. Embrace the amazing opportunity, and awesome responsibility, the universe has entrusted to you. In doing so, you will find your path to happiness in life broadened, and more clearly marked.

Jungian Self-Objects

Some students of the psychological theories of Carl Jung use the term *psyche* to stand for the totality of the mind, both conscious and unconscious.

We can define our conscious mind as that part of our mental process we are capable of monitoring: The thoughts we are having, and the emotions we are feeling. However, it seems there is another level of the mind: the unconscious, which we can usually only recognize from its secondary effects on conscious thinking but nonetheless operates continuously, out of our awareness. For example, as we have described it objectification is largely an unconscious process.

Jungians sometimes personify the psyche, and say things like: "Psyche is moving us in this direction.", or "sending us this message". This is simply a matter of taste, as the same ideas can be expressed in impersonal terms if we wish.

By definition, the workings of the unconscious mind cannot be monitored directly, but they can sometimes be inferred from observing behaviors or your own thoughts. Observing "Freudian slips" is one method, Carl Jung developed a method of noting pauses in word association tests. As I understand it, Dianetics uses changes in galvanic skin resistance to find unconscious associations to particular words or ideas.

The analysis of dreams is another, generally more accessible way of discovering more about our unconscious mental processes. Carl Jung, Sigmund Freud, and others have suggested that dreams offer a window into the unconscious through our conscious memory of them, and my own experience has validated this approach.

The *Inner Child,* the *Anima or Animus,* and the *Shadow* are distinct psychological constructs, self-objects, which seem to be present in all of us, and show up in dreams quite frequently. They can also be recognized in our impulses and compulsions, once we have developed an awareness of them.

I bring them up because it is very important for you as a parent to be aware of these psychological "entities" within you, since very often we confuse these self-objects with the object model of our actual external child. When this happens, there are unfortunate consequences for both you and your child.

The Inner Child

Briefly, the inner child is a lingering aftermath of your psychological state in childhood. Here lives on the openness, optimism, and joy of exploration, which may have been buried in the adult consciousness, but also the traumas, disappointments, and yearnings of your childhood as well. In dreams, this entity (or "complex" in Jungian terms) will often be represented as a child, and much can be learned about yourself from considering dream images of children from this point of view.

Sometimes, following the suggestion of a dream, you can reactivate and reconnect to this usually unconscious part of yourself by picking up an old hobby or passion, such as art or music or sport. By doing so, you can experience renewal, and a rekindling of the joy of living, as your inner child is allowed to manifest and have "its" desires met.

When a parent dreams or daydreams about a child, however, the image will often be in the form of their actual child (as a result of projecting their inner child onto their actual child). Thus, you might dream about your child ice skating beautifully, for example, when the dream is actually meant as a representation or reflection of your inner child.

This projection explains the behavior of many mothers and fathers who push their children so hard in the areas of music, acting, gymnastics, sport, or even school. Things that they were involved with as a child, or wished they had been. They project the needs or disappointments of their inner child onto their real children, but often they completely disregard the actual wishes or proclivities of their real child in doing so, oblivious to their mistake. Needless to say, this is often very damaging to a child, who is forced to sacrifice their own path of self-development in order to obtain the approval and acceptance of their parent.

What should happen in these circumstances is that the parent reconnects with music, acting, gymnastics, a sport or school or whatever attracts them, while letting their child choose for themselves what they want to explore, or continue to develop, as much as possible. In this way, both parent and child continue in their individuation (a Jungian term, roughly meaning "your own path"). In the usual case of confusion between the two inner object models, individuation of both parent and child is unfortunately stymied, unless by some random stroke of luck, their child is actually drawn to whatever the parent is drawn to as well. However, even in this case, if their child does not perform exceptionally or "make it to the top", they will feel the disappointment of the parent, and integrate it as their own inadequacy. The parent too, will never be satisfied with the achievement of their child; because what they actually need, to find satisfaction, is to work through whatever it is *themselves*.

As an example, I can offer the case of a former patient of mine whose father was a high school sports star, and later went on to make his living in a sport-related field. The son also enjoyed this sport, but at some point chose to make a career in the arts. The son struggled with the persistent feeling he had disappointed his father, and that his father disapproved of him. This kept him from having a close relationship with his father in later life, and from performing to the best of his ability in his chosen career as well.

An acquaintance once confided to me that she had completed medical school and became a doctor in order to please her parents, only to find after many years of schooling, and going deep into debt, that she really did not enjoy being a doctor, but was forced to remain one because of her financial obligations.

Another former patient was a highly successful business professional, who at one point in life had been a promising classical pianist in a prestigious music school. In the face of some initial criticism, he left that path to go into a "traditional" profession. In the process of attempting to reconnect with his inner child, I found out that his daughter was required to practice piano for at least an hour daily, in addition to doing her homework. We processed this situation, and while his daughter was quite good as a pianist, when the question came up as to whether she was practicing because she loved it, or because she knew it was a way to have his approval and attention, he abruptly left the analysis.

The Anima, Animus, and Shadow

We are fascinated by what we are not. Weak and strong, masculine and feminine, introvert and extrovert, rich and poor; our opposites fascinate us, causing either attraction or repulsion depending on genetic programming, or previous conditioning regarding what is acceptable socially.

In Jungian psychotherapy, an attempt is sometimes made to bridge these underdeveloped aspects of ourselves, in order to bring a sense of wholeness or richness to our conscious life, and to broaden our sense of who we are and what we are capable of.

In everyday life however, people tend to constrain themselves to familiar patterns of thought, feeling, and behavior, and project the undeveloped yet fascinating aspects of themselves onto other people, to whom they find themselves either attracted or repelled.

In Jungian analysis, we sometimes interpret dreams as messages from the unconscious (or Psyche) to our conscious minds, suggesting areas for exploration and development in pursuit of greater conscious wholeness, and sometimes areas to avoid.

In this framework, we often see the anima or animus, and sometimes the inner child, as personifications of Psyche in dreams that draw us in new directions. The shadow is the personification of those things that repel or terrify, but are nonetheless part of us.

When our unconscious is seeking to draw us to new areas, it chooses as symbolic messengers figures that are attractive. For heterosexual males, the figure is frequently female, which we call anima. For heterosexual females, the figure is often male, the animus. For an older adult, the figure may additionally be a younger person or child, and vice-versa, since older and younger tend to attract each other.

Since parents are usually attracted to their children, Psyche will often use your children in dream images as anima or animus figures, which creates a psychological confusion in the same way as when the inner child is presented in a dream.

In both cases, however, the message is the same. Psyche is calling you to make a change, develop something that was left behind, or explore something new. It is very often not a message for, or about, your actual child.

Whether from the uninformed interpretation of their dreams, or because of unconscious impulse, it is unfortunately common, almost universal, for parents to project their own inner child or anima/animus (desires and aspirations) onto their children. The fact that it is common does not make it appropriate. With awareness, this can be prevented, and the parent's wants and needs can stay with the parent, where they belong. Keep the desires and aspirations you have for your child as open-ended as possible: such as wanting them to be happy, competent in what they choose, confident, and caring. Support them in choosing their own road, as you discover new possibilities for your own development.

Unfortunately, sometimes parents project shadow onto their child. In my experience, this tends to occur when a child is a product of rape, or incest, or is unwanted for whatever reason. When this happens, the results are horrific, as evil, terror, and rage are projected onto a small, defenseless being.

Innate Drives

In the workings of the mind as I have described them until now, there are mental objects that are created to describe and model the external world, and mental objects that personify aspects of the unconscious. However, there is another aspect of the psyche to which we now turn our attention: innate drives.

As part of our genetic inheritance, we are all affected by certain impulses and desires, which arise irrespective of our external experience, though they are certainly modified and shaped in expression by that experience. The exact listing of these universal drives is a matter of ongoing research and dispute, but here is an informal list that will do for now:

Primarily biological urges:

To survive
To breathe
To drink
To eat
To sleep
To urinate
To evacuate
To maintain a comfortable environment
To engage in sex

Primarily psychological urges:

- To survive
- To be secure
- To belong to, be part of, a social group
- To be independent, free
- To seek novelty (curiosity)
- To understand
- To control (power or domination)
- To possess
- To destroy
- To create
- To nurture
- To be needed, have meaning
- To wholeness (expansion of consciousness, integration of opposites)

Many of these drives are interrelated and overlapping. The urge for security might be understood as a muted form of the urge to power or control, and as an aspect of the urge to survive (or vice-versa). The urge to destroy could arise from the urge to possess and control. That is, destruction is a way of controlling things which otherwise cannot be controlled, or of possessing things which otherwise can't be possessed. On the other hand, destruction can be an act of curiosity (seeking novelty), or power. Creation can also be seen as a combination of seeking novelty and power.

In addition, biological urges are often associated with psychological urges, and vice-versa. Sexual behavior is a great example of this, where the biological urge to engage in sex is for different people associated with the urge to control, the desire to be needed, security, the urge to seek novelty, or the urge to wholeness.

Because of conditioning, innate urges or drives are channeled and shaped into socially acceptable outlets - which correspond to internal object models. For example, the idea that sex is appropriate in marriage and not elsewhere is a common construct. Destruction is appropriate in war, or in a wrecking yard. Eating is appropriate in certain places, in certain ways, and at certain times. I visualize these models or constructs as "containers" for the urges they allow expression for, and the urges themselves as a sort of moving fluid, like water from a hose. Depending on genetic inheritance, previous conditioning, and the current situation, everyone has some given level of these urges, which need to find expression or outlet in some way.

To repeat, these drives and impulses are normal and expected parts of every healthy human being's experience.

Note however, that Psyche is not necessarily bound by the conditioning of our conscious mind, so dreams and impulses sometimes arise that are quite distasteful. The socially condoned containers we have created to channel our drives may not be broad enough, strong enough, or flexible enough to contain a particular drive or urge. When that happens, there can be uncontrollable "breaks" in those containers, and dangerous or harmful behaviors can result.

There are people with very strong urges to dominate or destroy for example, which are not well contained, and so they "take it out" on close family or friends, or less powerful people or animals they are able to manipulate or control. Similarly, some with strong sexual urges who have been conditioned or taught that masturbation is wrong, unmanly, or unfeminine, will turn to risky or harmful ways of satisfying their urges.

Psyche uses sexual activity or desire in dreams as a marker for the anima or animus. That is, sexual desire or activity in a dream, or even in normal consciousness as a passing thought, more often indicates a need to integrate some trait or characteristic that the dream sex partner has, and not a need to have sex with that person in real life. Sexual union is used by the unconscious as a symbol for the psychological urge to wholeness, or union with the opposite.

Unfortunately, some people with strong sexual urges project anima or animus onto children, and find themselves attracted sexually to them. Depending on the strength of the projection, they may have the delusion that children are sexually attracted to them as well. It is important to be aware of the projection, in order to protect the child.

Just as the urge to violence or anger directed towards a child (which is an expression of the innate urge for dominance, control, and aggression) must be re-interpreted, any feeling of sexual attraction or desire directed towards a real child, or the perception that a real child is sexually attracted to you, should be understood to be a projection and interpreted symbolically. That is, your unconscious is suggesting a need to become more childlike in some way.

Much of Transformative Parenting™ is about breaking or loosening artificially imposed boundaries on thought and action by following the naturally inquisitive lead of your child. However as an exception to the rule, the innate drives of dominance, violent aggression, and sexual behavior, must be controlled; and boundaries carefully imposed. As in all parent-child learning, the best way of teaching is through calm and patient example.

As a further caution, let me share that in my experience as a psychiatrist, children who have been treated as sexual objects by adults carry permanent psychological scars.

Even when they realize they were not in control of the situation, and should not feel responsible for what happened, they struggle with continuing feelings of guilt and shame. Often, because of behaviors that arose as their needs as children were manipulated and exploited, they worry they might have induced the abusive behavior on some level.

Among other things, they struggle as adults with trusting anyone, even themselves, and are at higher risk for abusing others as they themselves were abused.

It is has also been my experience that many adults who abused children in the past carry ongoing feelings of guilt and shame as well.

Given the problems adults have limiting their expression of inherent drives to socially acceptable containers, it should be no surprise that children, who have not yet formed containers, will sometimes express these urges in ways that can embarrass and shock unprepared adults. It is important to prepare ourselves in advance for these events, so we don't act in ways which might damage others, ourselves, or our child.

Try to treat these events matter-of-factly, without undue emotion. Strong negative emotional displays by parents will mark events in the mind of a child, and can create persistent feelings of shame or anxiety about normal urges that are very difficult to remove.

Try to help your child find outlets for their urges that are safe for everyone, yet allow for their individual needs. By doing so, you will find it easier to do the same for yourself.

Practicing Transformative Parenting

Remember that we want to remove faulty conceptual programming in ourselves, while minimizing the creation of incorrect programming in our child.

I have discovered two main practices to help us, achieve these goals.

First, is the practice of observing and re-interpreting negative emotion, which I paraphrase from our earlier discussion:

In interactions with your child, note the arising of negative emotions such as anger or disdain. Realize that the cause of your emotion is not wrong action by your child, but faulty expectations on your part. Correct those faulty expectations and re-address the situation calmly, patiently, and with new understanding.

I also offer another practice, which is difficult, but can be done during the hopefully lengthy periods when you are not unhappy with your child, and will take your process of transformation to another level:

While maintaining an empathic connection to your child, and simultaneous awareness of your inner emotional state and the external environment, strive to provide your child with the illusion of empowerment, even omnipotence; bounded only by empathic concern for others and the carefully considered limits of your actual, in-this-moment circumstance.

You can look at this exercise as a combination of David Winnecot's suggestions for the "good enough mother", Sigung's "Method of No Method", Sifu's instructions to me for assuring Sigung's well-being while in public, and the powerful practice of a disciple attuning themselves to their spiritual master.

We use as a marker of our success the expression of joy, happiness, or satisfaction on our child's face or in their body language. When those expressions are present, we are doing well, when they not, we are off track.

Accept this as a "best efforts" practice. Sometimes it will seem easy, and other times extremely challenging. It is in the frustrating parts that learning (and unlearning) take place, while when things are going well there is the feeling of shared joy. Disappointments and failures are inevitable, expected, and should be acknowledged calmly, in accordance with the goal of maintaining a "bubble" of security around your child. Note that it is necessary to feel secure before one can feel omnipotent, or even happy.

The frustration this practice often causes may well trigger negative emotionality, which should be dealt with in accordance with the first practice. Anger, and cold dismissal - which is often anger masquerading as calmness - represent breaks in empathic connection and should be considered signals that our inner object models or some aspect of our methodology needs to be adjusted.

While calm happiness is a good sign we are achieving our objective, joyful emotionality is even better, and should be allowed even at the expense of calmness. If quiet is necessary in the local environment, say at a movie, or at worship, see if you can go somewhere else to play for a while and allow your child to express their joy. Perhaps while you are at it, you can express your joy!

As a parent, remember we are engaged in a path of self-discovery and self-mastery as well as parenting. Practice in maintaining awareness and empathic connection furthers self-control and self-discovery, and the ability to "read" others non-verbally. Learn to manipulate the environment to maintain a space of calmness, and provide the illusion of empowerment, even omnipotence for your child. This is not only good for your child, but develops your own internal and external mastery as well.

For a child, having the experience of sustained empowerment allows them to incorporate into their core, inner self-object model the attribute of calm self-assurance, and reinforces their natural traits of inquisitiveness and desire to learn about and control their environment. This will ultimately lead to a calm, confident, independent, and knowledgeable adult.

When the inevitable disappointments occur, they will be caused by either a failure to understand the desires of your child, actual external limitations and requirements, or triggering of your negative emotions. If negative emotions, failures of understanding, or simple disregard for your child's wishes are rare, they will learn the actual boundaries of their existence; not artificially created or arbitrarily imposed ones. In addition, experiencing your ongoing, calm love, despite their expressions of frustration, will enhance the development of confidence, resilience, and persistence in the face of temporary defeat, and will do the same for you as well!

As parents, struggling to maintain our child's illusion of omnipotence as we struggle with our negative emotional responses, brings awareness of our perceived limitations and cultural restraints, and provides an opportunity to re-evaluate and potentially discard them.

Even when you cannot sustain the illusion of omnipotence, your child is aware of your effort. This supports your child's belief that you understand them (or are trying to), love them unconditionally, and are doing your best to make them happy. Moreover, this intensifies the love and respect your child has for you (though it may not be apparent in the moment of disappointment!).

In general, I recommend your initial response when you recognize a need or want in your child be "Here it is.", or "Yes, go ahead. I'm happy to help if you need me to." depending on their age, inclination, and capability. Use your knowledge of the world, and your child's enthusiasm, to figure out how to make it happen; while protecting your child's safety and respecting the boundaries of others.

I perceive this to be in contrast to the approach of most parents; which is to run the proposed action through a series of personal and cultural filters, looking for any excuse to give the hair-trigger response of: "No, you can't.", perhaps followed by, "Do this instead."; in other words, teaching fearful caution and rule-following, not mutual discovery.

This practice is not simply giving a child everything they want; though to the uninformed, it might appear that way. “Spoiling” a child is giving them whatever they think they want without attention or care. I have had patients whose parents were wealthy, but had little time for them as children. They instead “showed their love” by buying them things, giving them “whatever they wanted”. What they needed, and likely wanted most, was the loving attention of their parents. In my experience, children such as these grow up to have emotionally painful or empty lives, despite the wealth passed on to them by their parents. Monetary wealth does not equate to emotional wealth.

Though most parents’ instinct is to attempt to train and shape their child too strictly, there are some parents who swing too far the other way. I have noted this with some of my wealthy patients, whose parents raised them with the credo of avoiding disappointment at all cost. For most parents this is not a practical concern, because reality and circumstance provide more than enough boundaries and challenge to provide focus and direction for the parent and child, but for the wealthy, and particularly those with inherited wealth, the lack of boundaries and challenge in childhood can lead to dysfunction and chronic dissatisfaction in later life. For these parents Transformative Parenting™ is just as important. The challenge of sustaining an empathic connection, and commitment to their child’s well-being, gives direction to the parent’s life. Searching for and acknowledging appropriate boundaries based on empathic concern for others will help shape a positive self-image and persona in both the parent and child.

It is a reality of life that some parents have more material resources than others do, and therefore the material opportunities available to their children will be greater. On the other hand, some parents will have greater abilities in attunement or emotional control, or the ability to show love. What is important are not the material things that are provided by the parents, as much as the development and maintenance of the empathic parent-child connection, and the content of the messaging conveyed through this connection.

In the very early years with which we are primarily concerned here, even those with few resources should be able to sustain the illusion of omnipotence. For a small child, this comes when a bottle or breast magically appears when they begin to feel hungry, a diaper is changed when they first notice they are wet, they become cool and comfortable when they were hot, or warm and comfortable when they were cold; the environment becomes calm when they want quiet, they are held when they want holding, or let go when they want to explore.

While I believe empathy and compassion are extremely important qualities in an adult, they cannot be taught at an early age except by modeling appropriate behavior yourself. Don't try to "teach" empathy by forcing sharing for example, unless it is a necessary compromise due to empathic consideration for another child. Doing so simply breaks your empathic connection. However, do your best to try to figure out some way both children can be happy. Teach sharing by sharing with your child and with others. When they are older, they will emulate your example.

> *"Children have never been very good at listening to their elders, but they have never failed to imitate them." - James Baldwin*

It is not developmentally reasonable for a two or three year old to be sympathetic towards others. You simply force a disconnection in your empathic bond with them, and they feel alone, powerless, and afraid. Alternatively, they become angry, which is a secondary response or "defense" to the primary or initial emotion of fear. You actually demonstrate a lack of empathy when you try to force young children to empathize with others.

Speaking of forcing, do not make the mistake of forcing your child to attend to your needs, unless it is absolutely necessary. Attend to your child, not the other way around. If your child does not want to play with you that's fine, let them play with their toy, their friend, or however they would like. Even better, join with and assist them in what they want to do. If they insist on going it alone, you can enjoy a momentary break, or maintain your connection with them in order to appreciate the awesomeness of whatever they have discovered, or in case they eventually do need you to assist them, or they change their mind and want to play with you again. Be open to how they want to play, and do your best not to force your agenda on them. You can suggest, but do not force. Let your child experience the feeling of being empowered, even omnipotent, as much as you can.

Parents are a child's first and most constant teachers, and are therefore the most important in imprinting their child's primary object models.

The most powerful and effective teaching is through being a good role model. What you do is most important, what you say is way down the list. If you show your child empathy, and demonstrate empathy towards others when you are with them, they will learn empathy, or rather their innate empathic abilities will be developed fully over time. They will become caring adults; who empathize with others who are less powerful, because you empathized with them when they were powerless.

Parental Attributes

To reiterate, the two main practices of Transformative Parenting™ are:

1) *In interactions with your child, note the arising of negative emotions such as anger or disdain. Realize the cause of the emotion is not "wrong" action by your child, but faulty expectations on your part. Correct those faulty expectations and address the situation calmly, patiently, and with new understanding.*

2) *While maintaining an empathic connection to your child, and simultaneous awareness of your inner emotional state and the external environment, strive to provide your child with the illusion of empowerment, even omnipotence.*

Doing these practices will produce profound transformation in yourself, and promote healthy self-confidence, curiosity, and compassion in your child. I encourage you to begin practicing them with your child immediately.

However, I have found it is possible to enhance and enrich these practices by maintaining certain attitudes and developing certain attributes. This makes them easier, more effective, and more satisfying.

Helpful Attitudes

Transformative Parenting™ requires an attitude of respect for your child, but it is easier if you go further. Consider honoring and even idealizing your child as a teacher. If these you can do this, the other helpful attributes will come much more easily. It may be useful to remind yourself of this frequently at first, until it becomes second nature.

Culturally, most of us don't consider the lessons a child offers of any importance, which makes us unable to even perceive them. If we do not believe someone can teach us something, we cannot learn from them. A core part of most people's "learner" self-object is the presence of a teacher. Children can offer great wisdom, even though they require our care and assistance. It is understood that we must teach them, or rather, help them learn, as best we can; but this is best done carefully, with reverence and respect.

> *"Grown-up people do not know that a child can give exceedingly good advice even in the most difficult case."*
> *- Fyodor Dostoevsky*

Another helpful attitude is to consider your role as a parent to be similar to that of a regent. According to the dictionary, a regent is someone who governs a country when the king or queen is a minor. However, a good regent not only governs, they mentor the young queen or king, so they are ready and prepared to rule the kingdom wisely when they come of age. This is the stance I am recommending you take with your child. Honor them as prince or princess, understanding that one day you will step aside, and they will take over as ruler of their universe.

Your job is to mentor them for this sovereign role, protect them until they are ready, and step aside when that time comes.

A good regent is not stingy with the prince or princess. After all, you cannot learn about using great resources wisely unless you have practice with smaller resources. Similarly, they do not strive to control too tightly. You cannot learn how to handle great freedom wisely unless you have experience and practice with lesser freedom. You cannot learn how to be wisely powerful unless you have practice with power. A good regent is not stingy with resources, and not stingy with their time and attention. They take their job seriously, as one of great importance and responsibility.

Finally, a good monarch cares about the "common" people of his or her country. Thus, as regents, we gently teach empathy to the needs of others, primarily by being a good role model, and by gently correcting our child when they inadvertently hurt others by their actions.

A final helpful attitude is to look at the practice of Transformative Parenting™ as being a spiritual exercise. That is, to see it as a vehicle for your own self-development and growth. I know of no more powerful and effective way of discovering your own weaknesses and shortcomings, and learning to adapt to them, than following the path of Transformative Parenting™.

The Attribute of Attention

To create a feeling of omnipotence requires that a minimum of time elapse between the arising of a desire, and its satisfaction. For very young children who have short attention spans, this time is very short, on the order of seconds. To quickly satisfy your child's desires you must pay constant attention to them, unless they are asleep or engaged in an activity that you know from experience will satisfy them for some time.

This is hard work, and requires sacrifice. Cell phones, radio, housework, business, and social affairs must all be managed in a way that minimizes time spent away from being attentive to your child. When you are with your child, you should as best you can attend strictly to them. Otherwise, they learn they are secondary in importance to the cell phone, the computer, the TV (unless it is children's programming that they have requested), or even the broom or the mop for those parents who are excessive cleaners.

> *"A man should never neglect his family for business."*
> *- Walt Disney*

Of course, a balance must be struck which will be different for each parent. You need to provide for the security of your child (work, pay bills, clean the home), your own mental and physical health (exercise, hobbies, talking with friends, sleep), and attending to your child. Parents need help, and an occasional break, or both parent and child will suffer.

Attending to your child is its own practice, which will carry over into other life endeavors as improved concentration and focus. I have met numerous parents who have noted how much more they are able to get done in short periods of time since having children.

The Attribute of Emotional Control

Strong emotion, even uncontrolled love, is disruptive of empathic connection. Anger and disdain can destroy hope for the possibility of connection, and make later repair of the relationship that much harder. On the other hand, lack of emotion, felt as uncaring, is just as damaging.

In Transformative Parenting™ we use the presence of "negative" emotions as a signal to make us aware of conflicting inner object models. Noting these feelings is a positive in that sense. However, it is important to have the ability to note the arising of the emotion, mark the circumstances for further evaluation later, and then quell the emotion, or at least not act on it by striking, yelling at, or withholding affection from your child.

This quelling of emotion is not an easy thing for most people. Later, I will discuss some other, more general, practices for developing emotional control, but for now, consider this: It is very helpful to resolve in yourself ahead of time, that there is nothing a one, two or three year old could do or not do that would justify an adult being angry with them.

Do your best now to think up a situation where it would be justified to strike, yell at, demean, or hate a three or four year old child (actually any child). If you come up with one (or several), I ask you to take the time to analyze the surrounding situation now, in advance, and I believe you will find one or more errors in your models of children or the environment. See if I'm right. This is an opportunity for you to develop wisdom and reduce your chances of acting out inappropriately with your child.

Commit to not being angry "at" your child when you become angry in their presence. Then, when the emotion does arise, you can refer to your prior commitment, and it will be easier to let it go. Slowly counting to 50 while taking slow, deep breaths, is also a good basic exercise for bringing things into better perspective.

The Attribute of Empathic Attunement

Empathic attunement is the ability to align your thoughts and feelings with those of another person (reach a state of empathy). It is in some ways mysterious, and not easy for many people. Studies have shown that a small minority of people seem to lack empathy entirely, and so could be termed psychopathic. Note that all of these people are not criminals. Some find culturally accepted roles as businessmen, soldiers, policemen, lawyers and politicians for example. They lack the ability to feel what another person is feeling, though some are skilled in discerning others' emotions, faking empathy, and interpersonal manipulation. People affected by narcissism, Asperger syndrome, and some other conditions have a similar disability. In some ways, this is a good thing for them, as they are less susceptible to certain forms of projective identification, for example; but for a parent, it is a decided weakness. Even in the majority of people however, empathy can be “turned off” by reinforcing an object model of some person or group as being “less than” or “inhuman”. This is why the Nazi’s in World War II Germany were able to justify doing the most inhumane and cruel things to others without having to feel too badly about it. Without empathy, they had no perception of the pain they caused others. The same is true for slave owners, human traffickers, and all those who exploit or subjugate others today and in the past. As an aside, it is a cruel irony that mirror neurons, which may be the neurologic mediators of empathy, were discovered during experiments with a non-human primate, and not in Homo sapiens.

Empathic attunement is an extremely useful skill, which enables a parent to sense what their child needs or wants even when their child is pre-verbal, lacks suitable vocabulary, or is unable to verbalize their desires or concerns for whatever reason. Since providing a feeling of empowerment for your child is one of our goals, knowing what they want is obviously a necessary first step. Empathic attunement provides us this information.

Empathic attunement is gradually developed in childhood by interacting with empathic adults, particularly parents, and empathic older children. It can then be further developed or suppressed in adulthood. For parents of newborns, I have discovered a special second chance to re-learn and enhance empathic attunement. I call it *vibrational attunement,* and we’ll discuss it in detail later.

For all parents though, it is very important to spend time learning about the body language of newborns and infants.

Doing so allows you to show empathy, and provide the feeling of connected and understood, which is so important for the development of a sense of security in your child. We will have more to say about infant body language later on as well.

Developing Emotional Control

Over time, and as a result of my professional experience as a psychiatrist and psychotherapist, I have come to realize how few people have a reasonably good ability to self-monitor and self-regulate their internal physical and emotional state. This is perhaps not surprising, given the external, image, and material orientation of our modern society. It is nonetheless a problem if we are going to attempt a path of self-mastery that requires us to be self-aware so we do not confuse our various inner object models with themselves, or with external reality, or most particularly with our child.

Many people look at emotional states (feelings) as something different from thoughts or body sensations, but they are inextricably intertwined. Eckhard Tolle says: "Emotions are your body's reaction to your mind." If you pay careful attention whenever you experience a strong emotion, you can sense the body reactions that coincide with that emotion. For example, when you get angry your heartbeat and breathing rates increase, both of which are aspects of your sympathetic nervous system being activated. However, with anger you might also notice your fists and jaw clenching, and perhaps some other body reactions peculiar to you. With anxiety, many people experience tightness in their abdomen, or chest, or shoulders, or head (which can lead to severe headaches). People tend to carry anxiety in particular places most of the time, which can lead to chronic physical problems if the anxiety is not recognized and dealt with.

However, this mind-body connection has a two-way directionality: If you can consciously relax your tense jaw and fist, and slow your breathing, you will find that your angry feelings and thoughts begin to subside. We experience the converse of Tolle's statement. Emotions are also your mind's reaction to your body!

It is useful to note that our emotional state and the states of those around us are closely related. Observe how being around someone who is happy, sad, excited, or angry tends to induce the same emotion in you. This happens constantly and we are mostly oblivious to the effect, but it is the cause of much of the stress in our lives.

The same thing happens in reverse; the emotions we feel, we radiate to others, and if they are receptive or open to those emotions, they feel them as well. In fact, we can become angry if this does not happen when we expect it, because we perceive it as a lack of sympathy for our situation.

An unfortunate case is when we are upset, and pass that on to our child. Children are extremely sensitive to the emotional state of their caregiver, and will often respond with corresponding emotion.

We then blame our child; perhaps even punish them for being upset or acting out, when we or someone else is the cause.

Another sad case is when a parent becomes upset about something, and their child fails to understand that they are expected to become upset as well. Sometimes children are punished or shamed for being uncaring in this case as well!

This is why it is so important to maintain an inner and outer attitude of calm when in the presence of your child. You can and should be sympathetic to them when they are upset, but you should strive to remain calm while doing so, remembering that calm is not the same as distant, distracted, uncaring, or cold.

So, how can we use this understanding of the bi-directional mind-body connection to help us stay calm? I find it most helpful to address the issue from both directions: Mind or thinking, and its impact on felt emotion, and body tension with its effect on emotion. After all, what is emotion, other than a set of thoughts associated with a set of body sensations?

If we can calm our thoughts, and relax our body, we induce calmness, displacing whatever emotion was there before.

I am offering you two complementary practices to help you learn to self-induce a state of calmness: Progressive Relaxation, and Mindfulness. There are many others I am aware of, but I am forcing myself to be very selective. Both practices require time and effort to become effective, but the effort pays off when you find yourself able to remain calm in formerly difficult situations.

Progressive Relaxation

My practice of monitoring and attempting to control inner emotional and physical states began when I was around eight years old. We had recently moved to a house near the center of town, which had a basement filled with books left by the previous occupants. My bedroom was there, and I spent many hours perusing and reading those books.

One of the books I read most carefully was an old paperback about developing the ability to relax. For some reason, I was drawn to this book, and the exercises in it.

Over time, and with repeated practice, I found myself able to relax physically in most any situation, quickly and at will. I found this ability to be very useful and it became something of a reflex, which I used whenever I felt anxious or in danger. It has also formed the unconscious core of my later work with various forms of prayer, meditation, self-hypnosis, and spiritual practice. During the writing of this book, the memory of that time, and that book returned, and I would like to share what it taught me with you, so you can benefit as I have.

Progressive Relaxation is the method the book taught, and I believe it is the most useful starting point on the path to internal awareness and control, simply because it offers results more quickly than other methods. It has served me well for many years and through many tense situations.

It offers increased sensitivity to body sensations and tensions, the ability to relax the muscles of your body at will, and the ability to slow breathing and often the heart rate. Through the body-mind connection we discussed earlier, you get enhanced emotional control as well. There are no religious overtones to get in the way, and so few barriers for most people to attempt and practice it.

Edmund Jacobson, M.D. (1888-1983), who spent much of his career researching physical tension and relaxation techniques, developed Progressive Relaxation. He wrote the book *Progressive Relaxation* in 1929 and *You Must Relax* in 1934. The latter was probably the book I found in my basement.

As I mentioned before, along with the ability to physically relax, the technique allows for the development of a corresponding ability to emotionally relax. In addition to reducing overall stress levels, practice can eliminate the need for anti-anxiety medications, and create overall feelings of well-being and calm. The ability to maintain calm in the face of stressors which others find intolerable can be very useful in projecting an aura of self-confidence. In younger days, I would sometimes find myself in situations which were close to violence, and I believe my ability to remain calm warded off many potential attacks, not to mention enhancing my ability to handle myself more effectively on those occasions when a fight was inevitable.

For parents, it is extremely helpful to model calmness for their children, which they in turn incorporate into their own self-object. Also, the ability to remain calm when your "buttons are being pushed" allows you to be self-observant, and learn where you have a sensitivity so it can be analyzed further. This protects you from acting or reacting unconsciously out of fear, shame, or anger.

Unfortunately, the information I am about to give you seems to have been broadly overlooked and forgotten. You Must Relax was last printed in 1978. When I Google "Progressive Relaxation", it seems much of the material is historical, and even wrong. The non-profit National Foundation for Progressive Relaxation, which he founded, no longer exists.

Since his books are no longer in print, I will teach you his method here. Please read this over a few times before beginning your practice, to be sure you understand the method. I am condensing an entire book into a few pages.

The Jacobson Method

Jacobson described daily practice sessions of an hour or so. For most adults this is not practical, so just do the best you can and don't worry about it. Initially, lying down on your back (supine) is the best posture, as it allows for full relaxation of most of the body's skeletal muscles, which are the ones under voluntary or conscious control. Jacobson claimed that by relaxing the skeletal muscles completely, other non-skeletal, involuntary muscles, such as those involved in digestion for example, would also relax: though it took weeks or months of regular practice for that to happen.

The beginner's practice has two aspects: Learning to perceive muscle tension, and learning to remove it by consciously relaxing the tense area. By focusing our attention on a particular muscle or muscle group and inducing tension in that muscle group, we can learn what muscle tension feels like. Then we relax the muscle group, observe the effect internally, and maintain the relaxed state.

We finish each practice period by attempting to relax our whole body for a while.

As you progress, creating tension in a muscle first is not required. It gives the beginner practice in perceiving what "tenseness" in a muscle feels like, so they can better recognize the difference between "tense" and "relaxed". Once internal sensitivity has been developed, you can simply "go limp" without having to consciously tense a muscle beforehand. However, most people have poor internal sense of their individual muscles, and it can take quite some time for sensitivity to develop, so first inducing muscle tension will be very helpful initially.

Begin a practice by lying down on the floor or a mat. Place a shallow pillow or pad under your head, and perhaps a thicker one under the knees, as you lie on your back. Jacobson recommended keeping your arms to the sides, your hands not touching, and your legs uncrossed. He felt this would minimize "disagreeable" sensations from distracting you, but find for yourself the right supports and positioning to suit your particular body. It is best if the room is darkened and quiet. Try to block off some time so you are not expecting any interruptions.

Then, taking your time, gradually close your eyes. Avoid watching the clock; allow your internal clock to estimate when to move on to the next part of the exercise, or finish up.

Once your eyes have closed, spend a few moments generally relaxing your body and getting yourself comfortable. Then, begin working with the muscles you have decided to practice with that day.

The muscles he recommended working with first are the left wrist extensors. Tense these by bending your left hand at the wrist, so your fingers point up and away from you if you are lying down on your back and your elbows are slightly out. Hold this position for some minutes, and you will become aware of a vague sensation in your upper forearm. This is the sensation of muscle tension. Once you recognize the sensation, you can then relax those muscles by letting your hand fall limply. Note what the absence of muscle tension feels like. Repeat these actions a few times, each time holding the tension and relaxing for a few minutes. Do the same with your right arm. Note also the sensation called "strain", which is *felt in the wrist* while "tension" is being *felt in the muscles* of the upper forearm. Strain is felt in ligaments and tendons, tension is felt in muscles. Then, spend the final half of the session relaxing the whole body, muscle group by muscle group. As we noted before, it will be helpful at first to induce tension in a muscle group so you can isolate it perceptually. Notice that relaxing is not simply holding still, which most people do in a stiff way, using lots of muscle tension. Work on being "limp".

In the next session, begin with focused observation of the wrist flexors. Tense these by bending your hand at the wrist, in the opposite direction from the flexors. In following sessions, begin with the elbow flexors and extensors, the shoulder muscles, the lower and upper leg muscles, the abdomen and back muscles, the chest muscles, the neck muscles, and the skull and facial muscles. Finally, the muscles surrounding the vocal chords and the eye muscles are trained by noting tension in various positions and then relaxing it. After working with all these muscle groups, you will be able to go quickly into full body, deep relaxation and without having to induce tension first.

Supplement the supine practice by performing what he called *differential relaxation* during everyday activity. This involves seeking out muscles that are tense, but not needed for what you are doing, say when you are standing, walking, running, or sitting. Then consciously relax the unneeded muscles. If you practice this enough, it will become a habit, which over time will transform you into a relaxed person!

Continued practice will enable you to induce rapid mental and emotional quieting, enjoy a much enhanced body awareness, and maintain an overall feeling of calm and mastery, which will positively affect other areas of your life.

Mindfulness

Mindfulness goes by many names, such as Meditation on the Breath, and Zen Meditation. I offer it here as a complement to Progressive Relaxation, though as a technique I believe it has less power to hone the attributes we are working on quickly. Nevertheless, if done regularly, over time it will help you gain a sense of internal mastery and calm. It also has the advantage of being easier to teach and describe.

In this practice, you sit upright in a quiet, comfortable place, either cross-legged on a pillow, or upright in a chair. Keep your eyes closed, or stare at a space on the floor a few feet ahead, or slightly downward.

The central point here is to monitor your breathing.

Do not try to change, think about, or criticize your breath, just "watch" or feel it. Attend perhaps to the rise and fall of your abdomen, or the sensation in your nostrils (try to choose one place to focus your attention). Note when your attention drifts, and gets caught up in a thought or a memory, a distracting object in the environment, or a discomfort in your body. When one of these things occurs, the exercise is to calmly note the occurrence of the distraction, without judgment, and then gently return to monitoring the breath with full attention.

That is all there is to it. It sounds deceptively simple, until you try it. To assist in keeping your attention off other thoughts, some meditation experts advocate counting your breaths, either to yourself or with beads, say up to twenty, and then repeating.

This practice among other things trains attention: the ability to stay focused on one thing. Other meditation practices make it a bit easier by using mantras or sounds, either aloud or internally, as aids. Either a random sound or a meaningful word are used, to somewhat different effect. Some endorse visualizing the breath as energy moving in and out of the body.

All of these techniques help you maintain focus or regain focus after becoming distracted. Nevertheless, when you are in a sufficiently calm mental state, I recommend you go back to simply monitoring your breath, perhaps occasionally experimenting with monitoring "everything" or "nothing".

Over time, intrusions of thought are less frequent, and easier to let go. Your mind calms, and emotionality is subdued. While this is mostly a practice about "being in the moment", as you prove to yourself the temporary, fleeting nature of thoughts and emotions, you become less attached to them. They hold less power over you.

These two internal awareness and control practices can be combined: After relaxing your skeletal muscles, attend to your breath.

Do not wait for a "perfect" time to practice either or both exercises. A few minutes on the train or on the bus are enough to do some differential relaxation and mindfulness breathing. Even a few moments, when you find yourself becoming anxious or upset, can be quite helpful.

Don't wait for a crisis, start practicing now. On the other hand, if you are in crisis, now is also the best time to start.

These two practices work in different ways to help us achieve our goal of being able to induce and sustain a state of calmness under pressure. This immensely useful skill enables us to maintain a protective sphere of calm empowerment around our child. In addition, as we grow more habituated to a state of calmness, we are able to recognize more quickly when we are at risk of "losing it". We become more sensitive to the conflicts in our object models, which in turn gives us the opportunity to recognize ever more subtle conflicts and correct them. Our journey of self-discovery will always lead to new discoveries.

Developing Empathic Attunement

Empathic attunement is critical to Transformative Parenting™ because it gives you the ability to intuit your child wants and needs. You can be attentive to your child, as say to a ball game, or your breath, but unless you attune, that is, actively see as they see, hear as they hear, and feel as they feel, it will be very difficult to give them the experience of omnipotence that will empower both of you.

In the absence of empathic attunement, it becomes much more likely the parents will substitute projections of themselves: their own wants and needs, for their child's wants and needs.

This is especially important for a pre-verbal child, but also for older children, when conditioned resistance (politeness, fear, shame, guilt) can get in the way of authentic verbal communication.

The development of empathic attunement with your child requires certain things. The first is receptivity on your part.

There must be a desire to understand and feel from your child's point of view. This requires, at a minimum, respect for your child, but is much, much easier if you can hold a feeling of reverence or devotion.

Admittedly, reverence is more difficult to sustain for the parent who was not fortunate enough to experience it themselves in their early childhood, but I encourage you to try as best you can. Your reward will be that much greater.

Secondly, there must be a channel or channels of communication. Later I will discuss a deep level of communication that may not be available to everyone, but universal channels do exist. These are mediated by the primary senses: Sight, sound, touch, and smell.

A surprise for many people is that children are communicating, or attempting to communicate, from birth. Here is a crash course in understanding your pre-verbal child:

Initially, children use eye movement and lip smacking to express their needs and desires. If they look at something, they are interested in it. If they look away, they are not. Consider they may be tired, frightened, or need a break to process things. They may be interested in something else.

Do not attempt to force your child to attend to a particular toy or even to you when they look away. If you do, you are disrupting their experience of omnipotence, inducing anxiety, and reinforcing feelings of powerlessness. Give them a moment to regroup. Shortly they may be interested again, or they may have moved on to exploring something else.

Infants will look at you for various reasons. If you are holding them, they may be content. If you are not holding them, they may want to be held quietly. They may want to be entertained, fed, or need help. Sometimes they want to know they have your attention, before looking at something else they want you to get for them or bring them towards to explore.

Likewise, they will look away from you for various reasons: They may want to explore something else, are tired, are afraid of you, or they want you to stop or change what you are doing. When your child looks away, at a minimum pause what you are doing, and try to understand why.

Later on, children develop more control over their facial muscles and neck, and will use them to indicate more clearly what they wish. Still later, they can point, hold, and push away objects. These movements all contain obvious meanings.

Lip smacking indicates a desire for a nipple, either because they are hungry, or to soothe themselves if they are over-stimulated and anxious. A breast, bottle, or pacifier should be offered, and/or a shift to a less stimulating environment (quieter, dimmer, less movement). Rapid smacking or sucking may mean higher anxiety or discomfort, slower indicates calm, content, or happy. Blowing can mean a desire to push away. If they spit out the nipple or pacifier, don't force it, there may be something wrong with the formula, or they need something else.

In terms of sound, there is of course crying, which indicates something is wrong, and cooing or babbling which indicates they are happy, often when exploring. An attuned parent will also learn early "words" their child creates for particular objects, which greatly enhances the feeling of connectedness. Don't be afraid to use these "words" with your child for fear they won't learn the "right" words later.

The ability to pronounce certain sounds develops over time, and cannot be forced.

Accept your child where they are, now. You will only be in this moment with them once. Let the experience be a happy one for both of you.

Touch is a very important channel of communication, though often neglected, or even rejected.

Your child needs your loving touch to give them the confidence to explore, and to assuage their fear of being alone and powerless. It is a natural need we share with all mammals.

How you hold your child sends information to them: that you are happy, angry, or sad; and if you are open to it, the reverse is also true. You can learn a lot about the state of a child from a clinging grasp, the squeeze of a finger, a push, or the pounding of a little fist.

The awareness of subtle movement a few times allowed me to tighten my grip on my child's ankle as she was about to take a "header" out of my arms and onto the ground! Try making your child the focus of your "mindfulness" practice, so your attention is on them and you are ready for the unexpected.

Explore the topic of early infant communication on your own. I will have a bit more to say on this topic later, but I can only scratch the surface with hopefully enough basics to start you off properly on your own path of discovery.

Vibrational Attunement

"There are more things in heaven and earth, Horatio, than are dreamt of in your philosophy."
- Shakespeare

As I alluded to in the introduction, my discovery of *Vibrational Attunement* was one of the motivators that led me to write this book. Though it may not be a practice available to all parents, I am including a description of it here for those who might find it helpful.

It is a bit scary to report something perhaps unique to me, but these things happened, and I feel it is important to speak up, and lend credibility to others who might share my experience in the present or future.

The birth of my child, and the period shortly thereafter, was a very stressful and exhausting time for me. Perhaps because I had more than an average amount of training in obstetrics and pediatrics during my residency, and therefore knew how things were "supposed to go", I was on high alert during the entire process. Unfortunately complications arose which threw me into "alert mode".

As a result, I got little sleep, and was slow to recognize, or perhaps misunderstood the feeling of drowsiness that came over me whenever I held our little newborn.

Nevertheless, at some point during the hospital stay I did recognize a kind of "sleep field" which surrounded her, especially when she was comfortably asleep in my arms.

I sensed this as a kind of vibrational field, which extended in my perception to at least a few feet around her, but was much more powerful when she was held.

Although I noted the existence of the field during our hospital stay, it was only after we got home, and the medical issues that activated me resolved, that I relaxed enough to think more about this discovery.

I considered that I might be imagining things, but to be frank the sensation was just too powerful to chalk up to imagination. I have created sensations and images in my imagination before, but for me the combination of the clarity and power of the sensation, along with its repeatability when getting near to my daughter and then moving away, proved to me the reality of what I perceived.

What I sensed, and what seemed to have the effect of inducing a pleasant drowsiness in me, was a powerful "vibration". I am not sure if you will be able to feel it with your own child, but I invite you to try. Imagine standing in front of a bass speaker at a rock concert as the music is playing, but wearing earplugs that completely mute the sound. This approximates what I was feeling, mostly in my chest and head.

For some reason, it occurred to me there might be a benefit to working with that vibrational energy in order to strengthen my attunement to her: and so I developed a practice of trying to harmonize with it.

I found the sensations to be quite powerful for about the first four months of my daughter's life, at which point they began to gradually decrease in strength. Somewhere around nine to ten months of age they became much more faint and difficult to sense.

Unfortunately, I do not know if some special parental sensitivity is needed here or not. I have not heard of anyone describing something similar before, and I have not done any polls or studies myself. I hope others will be able to replicate what I did, mostly because the process leads to a wonderful sense of connectedness with your child.

Perhaps the practice of Progressive Relaxation, Mindfulness, or other meditation practices can enhance people's internal sensitivity to a level where they are able to perceive these vibrations, where they could not otherwise. Visualization practices such as the Sufi *Five Element Breath,* which encourage the perception of inner energies, might be useful. On the other hand, perhaps this perception is actually a natural thing, which only needs to be attempted with an open mind, and practiced, - like breastfeeding for example.

I am going to describe the practice I came up with, in the hope it will bring you and your child benefit. If it does not work for you, do not consider it a big deal. People are born with different talents and sensitivities.

I sincerely believe you can become an adept practitioner of Transformative Parenting™ even if this particular exercise proves difficult. In any case, it may only available as a practice until your child is a few months old.

In general, I found this practice most easily done with my infant daughter asleep in my arms; while sitting in an easy chair, or lying down propped up at an angle with pillows. The vibrations resonated most powerfully when her head was near mine, and when I placed her so the crown of her head was tucked loosely to my throat. However, when she was very young I did not need to be specific in how I held her, as long as I was holding her.

As a newborn, the vibrations were powerful and jumbled, and induced a strong desire to sleep. I understood this to have a functional, evolutionary value; since sleeping with your child keeps you, their protector, in close proximity. Another benefit is that resting while your child is resting allows you to be more attentive and responsive to them when you are awake.

I believe when any parent sleeps with their child, or holds them with loving regard, attunement is taking place between them on an unconscious level, which strengthens the parent-child empathic bond.

However it may be possible to work at attuning to these vibrations in a conscious way, and doing so may allow you to perceive even more clearly what is going on with your child both psychically and physically. It may also offer opportunities to nurture growth and expansion, and sometimes even facilitate healing.

While recognizing that words are inadequate to describe what I did, my first attempts at attunement involved trying to shift my vibrational "pitch" to match or harmonize with hers, much like tuning a guitar by tightening or loosening a string to match the sound of another string.

I found these attempts to be unsatisfactory, because of the complex nature of the vibrational energies I perceived. Not only was the overall vibration "faster" than what I felt mine to be, it was actually a discordant combination of frequencies, which created a cacophony of vibrational noise that blocked any attempts to match it with conscious "tuning" of my own vibrational field, and in fact made it uncomfortable for me to try to do so.

The solution to this problem came to me in an elevator, where my gaze happened to rest on a wispy strand of dust, one end of which was stuck to the wall, the other floating free on an imperceptible current of rising air.

By observing that strand of dust, and the angle at which it floated out from the wall, I was able to detect the slightest shifts in the current of air that was supporting it. If the strand had been thicker, it would have simply hung down, but its lightness allowed it to reflect extremely subtle shifts in the surrounding air current.

A similar example is the resonating membrane of a microphone, where thinness and light mass allows the membrane to move in sympathy with the subtle sound vibrations striking it, mirroring the sound of your voice for example, with precision.

Although I cannot tell you exactly how, once I made an effort to "lighten" my own psychic state, I was able to "listen" to her vibrations and even allow them to permeate through me with much less discomfort than before. In fact, I eventually perceived it to be a cleansing and purifying experience to float lightly in her vibrational aura.

I believe sitting quietly in your child's vibrational field, whether you are conscious of it or not, with a light, open awareness, will attune you to them. Subtle channels of communication open, which allows you to sense their wants and needs more easily on a non-verbal level. This allows you to be a better caretaker, and for your child to feel safer, more secure, more loved and understood.

Conversely, your child's ability to sense your feelings and desires increases as well. It is my perception, though I have no proof, that infants are naturally sensitive to this vibrational energy, and this is an important way they have of understanding their environment.

Unfortunately for children, most adults present a jumbled and conflicting vibrational message (just as children do), accurately reflecting their conscious and unconscious conflicts. This leads many children to feel (in harmony with their parents) a nearly constant message of conflict, anxiety and insecurity.

However, you will find that as you continue in Transformative Parenting™ there develops a clarification of purpose, a resolution of conflicts, at least with respect to your child. This allows your message of love and support to be "heard" more clearly, without the background noise of conflicting motives and desires.

Psychic Healing

I believe with a deep level of attunement comes the possibility of sharing information and energies on a psychic or subtle-body level, and that doing so can assist in healing illness.

Psychic healing is a reality, though admittedly unreliable, at least at my skill level. Nonetheless, despite my limited experience, I would like to pass along my method, and some cautions, for those parents who find they are in a position to attempt it:

Begin in an attuned state. Thus, the two of you are physically together, in a quiet place if possible. You in a clear, open, calm, "sensing" state, and your child however they may be. One might think a strong emotion of love would be helpful, but for this particular exercise it is not. The feeling is there, but it must be contained and "risen above". Uncontrolled love can overwhelm, and pollute the neutrality which is essential for proper sensing of the subtle energies involved.

Begin by "embracing" your child's psychic energy field, in a calm measured way. Surround it but don't smother it. Then relax and merge, or blend with it. Lightly. Seek to not dampen or change your child's field in any way. To this point, we are essentially practicing Vibrational Attunement as I outlined above.

After you spend some time in this merged state, you may become aware of a discomfort in your body. This could be a sign of what is discomfiting your child. If you have been practicing Progressive Relaxation, you will be familiar with your own areas of chronic physical discomfort, and you will find it easier to distinguish what is new, and thus potentially a result of resonating with your child's discomfort.

Allow yourself to draw healing energy from the universe to that newly uncomfortable area in *your* body, perhaps on the in-breath. Allow this to go on for some time. It is possible you will reach a point where the discomfort goes away or feels partially resolved. Then start over, beginning again with attuning to your child, and embracing their energy field, or if you are tired, just be with them, and rest together.

That is how it is done.

Here, we are allowing the empathic bond between you and your child to act as a channel, to transmit your body's knowledge of how to heal the affected area, to your child's body, on a subconscious level.

In my opinion, it can be harmful to try to transmit healing energy "directly" to the affected part of your child, because of the numerous interdependencies between body subsystems that could be inadvertently disrupted, and our ignorance of the energies we are invoking.

By performing the healing in an indirect way, on ourselves, we admit our conscious ignorance of the "right way" to heal the situation, but we instead allow the subconscious wisdom of our adult body's experience in healing itself to be passed on to our child's relatively inexperienced body. Thus giving it an advantage in dealing with whatever pathogen or trauma it is confronting at this moment. As students of immunology know, the body learns over the years how to deal with more and more of the pathogens that constantly try to invade it. This is why older people get fewer colds than children do. With this healing practice, we are passing on some of this accumulated body-wisdom to our child.

Although controversial, at the end of a healing session, I have sometimes allowed for some "general" transfer of energy to my child. I have been taught by shamanic healers not to allow personal energy to pass to another when healing, because it can lead to unbalance and illness in the healer. So, perhaps this is a mistake, but with my own child I have certainly attempted it.

It is accomplished simply with a conscious willingness, while in an attuned state: "Take whatever you need." There will be a drain on your energy level, and perhaps you will get sick as well, but as a parent, I have willingly paid the price.

Sometimes high-level psychic healers attune themselves to high energy beings, such as angels, gods, ascended masters, Jesus, God, elementals, etc., and channel those being's energies for use in healing. My advice though, is to be cautious about these things.

Using the above technique, I have had the subjective experience of noting sinus infections, earaches, viral infections, and even a pyloric stenosis in my daughter, and have had the distinct impression of being of some help to her in all of those situations.

If you are not able to consciously attune to or enter a healing state with your child, a vast amount is still accomplished by gently holding or touching your child, (physical contact is important) and "sending" feelings of unconditional, no-strings-attached love and support to them: consciously while you are awake, and while you both nap. Prayer can have a similar effect, if your attitude is correct, and it is something you are comfortable doing.

These methods also activate ancient healing processes for your child's benefit.

Boundaries

I visualize a person's range of power, influence, and freedom to be like a bubble, or sphere, radiating outward. These spheres of freedom or empowerment vary from person to person, and from context to context, sometimes larger (less restrictions), and sometimes smaller (more restrictions).

For example, a wealthy person who might generally enjoy substantial freedom in many realms, would likely feel much more fearful and restricted if he or she suddenly found themselves walking alone in a bad neighborhood, than would a person who lives in that neighborhood.

For most of us, our spheres of power, influence, and freedom extend further than we realize. In other words, we have more freedom, influence, and power than we know.

I remember once walking with Sigung through a new-to-me, rather seedy section of Chinatown. He apparently sensed some level of discomfort in me, or perhaps projected it onto me, and told me: "Just act like you belong here, and nobody will bother you."

Sigung here pointed out what I am calling a boundary condition, noted by a sense of anxiety in either him or me. He then offered a solution: Act confidently, as if you belong here. By doing so, in short order I began to feel I did belong there, and whatever anxiety I (or he) may have felt was gone.

Transformative Parenting™, through its two major practices, similarly offers a way to reclaim some of our lost freedom, or sense of comfort and influence in the world, which we have lost due to faulty teaching and training, or wrongly interpreted experience.

The breaks in omnipotence your child experiences while you are attuned with them, or the arising of negative emotions in you, correspond to learned inhibitions or boundaries in one or more of your spheres of influence. You cannot move forward with something your child wants to do, because there is a learned rule that prevents it.

Some of these learned rules are valid, but if you take the time to re-evaluate them consciously, you will also find many are not.

Until around two years of age, given an ability to attune empathically, it should be possible for parents to provide their child with a reasonably consistent illusion of omnipotence. A young child's needs are usually not that complex or expensive. Attunement and willingness on the part of the child's caregiver are the main requirements. The relatively rare, necessary breaks in their illusion will come about mostly due to conflicts with other children over possession of desired objects, such as toys for instance.

However, for even the best parent, somewhere around the age of two, the illusion of omnipotence will begin to break down more frequently as their child's wants and demands begin to outstrip what is possible.

Whether breaks or boundary conditions occur before the age of two or after, how we handle these situations is very important.

Where it is clearly impossible to satisfy your child, it is important to make a real attempt to explain why. (i.e. the toy belongs to someone else, or they are too young to drive the car safely, or legally etc.)

Don't expect they will always understand and accept your explanation though. Many times, they'll still be very disappointed, sad, and upset with you. However, making the attempt is very important.

Tolerate their upset (and yours) calmly and with patient love. Note, while you do this, that you are modeling for them how to handle disappointment in the future when they are on their own.

Situations where it is possible for you to do something for them, but you want to encourage them to do it for themselves, can be problematic. In general, it has been my experience that children have a natural desire towards self-empowerment, and often get upset when we try to help, say, in the interest of time. Sometimes, there seems to be a test involved, but I don't think it's always the "test of wills" that many parents assume. Instead, I think it is sometimes a test of whether the parent still "has their back". In which case, allowing a mild regression might actually be emotionally empowering for your child.

> *"Sometimes you put walls up not to keep people out, but to see who cares enough to break them down."* - *Socrates*

Sharing Pain

The most important thing, when your child's feelings of empowerment must be disappointed, is the maintenance of your empathic connection. Sometimes in life, there are no easy answers, only hard choices. It is important that your child knows you are with them, feeling their pain. Here is an example:

Once, when my daughter was almost four, I went to pick her up from a play date with one of her friends. It was clear she'd had a great time, and was initially happy to see me, showing me all the cool toys they had been playing with, and the art they had created. However, her mood changed when I told her it was time to go. She scuttled away when I tried to put her socks and shoes on, and even punched me as I persisted. Eventually, after continued, repeated explanation that her friend had to get ready for a ballet class, and she had to come home to get changed for a swim class, and repeated attempts to hold her and her "getting away", she broke down sobbing and gave up resisting me getting her dressed to go outside. Then, I got her dressed and carried her home, as she cried with great, heaving, shuddering sobs. When we got home, I held her for a long while. Both of us were quite sad, and I apologized some more for having to take her away from her friend.

All in all a very painful experience for both of us, and that is the main point I am making here. Your child should know that it is painful for you as well. Not just because you say it, but because he or she can see it, hear it, and feel it in you.

You *should* feel your child's pain, as a direct result of your empathic connection, which should not be broken even when - especially when - it results in pain.

Transformative Parenting™ is a way of growth on multiple levels. I hope I have shown it to be a path of knowledge, which develops awareness on an intellectual level. Now I am showing you how it is also a path of the heart, which develops awareness and sensitivity on an emotional level.

There is in life inevitable pain and suffering, and most of us are accustomed to doing our best to ignore or hide from the pain and suffering of others. However, trying to escape or defend against the suffering of others (or even ourselves) hinders the expansion of awareness, and in the case of our children creates a disruption in our empathic connection; potentially causing them to feel alone, powerless, misunderstood, or unloved.

As I mentioned earlier, sometimes life presents us with hard choices. You can try to minimize suffering (and I recommend it!), but whatever you do, sometimes there is only suffering.

Take as an example a poor man who does not have money to buy food for his family. His friends have nothing, he has nothing, there is no job available for him to make money, and the government will not give his family enough to survive. Here, his only option to survive is to rob or steal. The boundary of not causing harm or suffering to others is in conflict with the innate drive to assure the survival of his family. Something must give, and genetic imperative will likely force the man to rob or steal so his family can survive, even if it means he will later go to prison or worse for it.

A similar situation arises with a child or young person who is in an abusive or neglectful home, and finds that in order to survive they must flee. They find themselves on their own, with no skills or resources. People in this situation will rob and steal, if they are strong enough, or prostitute themselves if they are not. The boundaries of self-respect, morality, and legality must give way to the genetic imperative to live.

These things happen. The most important thing is to acknowledge reality, maintain your connection to your child, and do your best for them. The position of the mother who has to flee an abusive relationship in order to protect herself and her child, yet has nowhere to go, is another example that comes to mind.

Sometimes there is no good answer now, but note that boundary conditions, meaning limits on you and your child's actions imposed by external reality, are not static. This is because external reality is not static, and you and your child's internal reality (meaning your potentials and capabilities) are not static. Thus, where there was a boundary in the past, there may not be now or a minute from now, or tomorrow or ten years from now. This is the basis of hope.

By the process of Transformative Parenting™, you discover with your child the true boundaries of your existence. The signal or sign that brings awareness of a potentially removable boundary is either a hesitancy to do as your child requests, or the arousal of an emotion such as anger, shame, anxiety, fear, or cold dismissal. When you note one of these, pause and consider: Is this a necessary boundary, or not?

If your signal is the arousal of anger or cold dismissal, there is definitely at least some aspect of false boundary involved, that is to say some invalid knowledge or conditioning that has been triggered, activating your mind's defenses around "being right".

If the sign is hesitancy, the boundary may be real or false, in other words valid or invalid, based on current circumstances. Based on your analysis of the situation, you may have the opportunity to confront this boundary and test its validity.

If the boundary is found to be valid, your challenge is to adapt to it while retaining as much freedom and power for you and your child as possible.

When a boundary is determined to be invalid, there is an expansion of your self-image through its removal, and the maintenance of your child's self-image of omnipotence. You will find this to be empowering and pleasurable for both of you.

If a boundary is tested and found to be real, you are forced to limit both your self-image, and your child's. This unfortunately, but necessarily, creates emotional pain. However, remember the basis of hope I mentioned above.

Many of the psychological boundaries you find will turn out to be imaginary, overblown, or the external realities underlying them are not quite where you thought they were. By letting your child take the lead, and allowing them to operate from their natural sense of omnipotence, you can together circumambulate the boundaries of Reality, and in the process recover a great deal of the power that you did not realize you had.

While it may initially feel like a limitation, following and "giving in" to your child is ultimately incredibly empowering for both of you.

New Boundaries

While practicing Transformative Parenting™ will often lead to the perception, testing, and removal of previously unknown boundaries to your freedom, your enhanced powers of attunement and empathic connection will also lead to the discovery of appropriate new boundaries.

As you continue the practice of empathic connection with your child, you will experience an increase in your empathic sensitivity to other beings. You will begin to feel their feelings as well.

Next comes an enhanced awareness of when your actions cause suffering in others, and finally a desire to minimize that suffering.

This discovery within you of the basis of *The Golden Rule,* is also incredibly empowering, though also disguised as limitation.

Odds and Ends

By now, you have a pretty good sense of Transformative Parenting™. In this chapter, I'm going to continue to stir the pot: to reinforce some things, to blend some of the ideas together, and perhaps bring some interesting tidbits to light.

Attitude

As I said before, attitude is fundamental. It can really help if you make the determination in advance that raising your child is the most important thing you can do with your life. This decision will greatly simplify many future decisions, and will positively influence your satisfaction with life later, as you age and come closer to death.

Becoming a parent means you must hit the "pause button" on many aspects of life, at least until your child no longer needs your constant attention. This becomes much easier if you truly feel your child and their development is of utmost importance.

Of course to engage in Transformative Parenting™ means you are learning an incredible amount anyway; but if you had been hoping to learn how to swim, play guitar, act on a stage, or fulfill some other childhood dream, be willing to take it slowly unless you have lots of support.

Commitment

Childrearing is a full time job and then some. To do it well takes great commitment. I understand that some are unable to make that commitment, but realize there is a price to pay for both of you. This is not to place blame or judgment, just acknowledging the facts of the situation. If you must work to pay the bills, which is understandable and necessary, it means you are not home offering security, support, empowerment, love, and guidance to your child; and you are not learning from them.

If it is necessary to be away from your child, do your best to find kind, loving caretakers. Nothing is more important.

Also, remember that if you are home but constantly on the phone, texting, on Facebook or Twitter, watching TV, or listening to the radio, you are showing your child that he or she is not as important as those things. You are not allowing them access to their greatest source of power: you. In addition, you are not accessing your greatest potential source of wisdom: your child.

It Takes a Village

You cannot do it all alone. It will become apparent quickly that you are human, and need time for yourself. You need rest, exercise, and your "inner child" needs attention. You need to be able to maintain social connections to friends and family. It is best if your spouse or partner can shoulder a share of the load. This is good for them, because it allows them time for actualization, self-development, and fun. It is good for your child, because he or she has the opportunity to learn from another perspective, and it is good for you.

If you are a single parent, do the best you can. Patience, one of the primary virtues of a parent, wears thin when you are tired. Rest when your child rests, and if you wake up first you will have a small break. Find opportunities for play dates with other children and parents. When your child is older and they do not require constant direct supervision, a trip to the playground can be a break.

When necessary, television can be a lifesaver. There are some very good children's shows nowadays (though too much of anything is not good). However, monitor what they watch, and minimize programs that shift scenes too frequently, contain lots of loud noises, or violent or scary situations. Calm educational programs like Sesame Street, Word World, and some others work best for toddlers.

Finally, remember that to be a parent is a blessing, even when it seems difficult. It is a gift many wish for, though often taken for granted, or even resented.

Learn About "Normal"

The greatest source of frustration I see with parents, which is translated into anger or disappointment with their children, and turns into negative self-esteem for the child, is a lack of knowledge about what constitutes normal age-appropriate development, and what can be expected of a child at a given age.

Parents sometimes make inappropriate demands of their children, where they are unable to comply because they are not physically or mentally able to, or previous conditioning interferes. Parents then make the mistake of thinking their child is being resistant, stubborn, or defiant, and push them harder, or punish them. Both the parent and the child are then likely to make the serious mistake of incorporating into their image or model of the child the idea that there is something "wrong" with the child.

A child does not come into the world with all its physical capabilities intact. It is often not simply about "learning how to do it". One example is potty training. There is actual, physical, post-birth neural development that needs to occur before it is possible for a child to learn to control their elimination processes.

This is true for psychological development as well. For example, it should not be expected that a child of two will be able to understand the concept of "sharing". I once watched a parent in the park withhold water from her daughter, telling her it had to be shared with her brother first (who was off playing elsewhere). The girl was quite traumatized by the whole thing, and it was clear to me she only saw that the mother was disregarding her thirst for water, while holding a bottle in front of her, and telling her that her brother was more important than she. Very sad.

When done carefully, teaching your child can be a good thing, but even better is to simply align yourself with your child and be encouraging, as their normal curiosity leads them into discovery, learning, and mastery.

Good Days and Bad Days

Our mastery of a new task is often of the "Two steps forward, one step back" variety. A child may do something once, then not be able to repeat it for quite some time. My mother told me I took six steps across a sofa at six months, and then did not walk again until I was a year old. That is probably extreme, but you get the idea. Do not demand something that your child is not capable of, just because they did it once.

Wives often tell stories of how their husbands turn into little whiny children when they get sick, and cannot do anything for themselves. Children do the same when they are sick, or tired, or hurt, or hungry. This is being human, and is not resistance or defiance.

Relax. Encourage, Don't Push

The best way to teach is by doing. Your child will observe your generosity with them and others, and will naturally mimic you when they are capable of doing so. They will watch you going to the potty, and when they are ready, you can be ready with encouragement and help.

Have on hand a good reference on child development. However, let me reiterate that your child should be the final educator for you on their development. Let them take the lead, and with your loving support they will move forward in their development as quickly as they possibly can. Trying to "push" a child before they are ready or interested is only counterproductive. It wastes your energy, and your child's, on something that is not ready to happen. It takes time away from other learning and exploration that your child wants to do instead, and turns you into an obstacle or adversary, instead of a source of love and support.

Conversely, if your child is interested in something, follow their lead. Encourage them and help them learn, even if the subject seems "too advanced".

Parental Drug Use

As a rule, recreational drug use (including alcohol) should be kept to a minimum, especially when you are around your child. Drugs eventually disrupt empathic connection: during the high, the withdrawal, or both. Depending on the drug used, they can reduce emotional and physical sensitivity, cause emotional volatility, and increase narcissistic tendencies. As drugs wear off, your body and mind need time to recover - your body feels tired, and your mood tends to become depressed and irritable. If drug use causes a marked change in behavior, it can be frightening for a child, as their parent becomes a potentially violent or neglectful stranger.

I say as a rule, because I have known emotionally volatile parents who used marijuana to mellow themselves. This allowed them to provide a sense of stability and calm for their children that they would not otherwise have been able to achieve. For a few people alcohol has a similar mellowing effect, though more often I find alcohol worsens emotional volatility.

Doing the practice of Transformative Parenting™ leads you to crave the clarity of awareness that comes with being drug-free, because it allows greater levels of attunement.

If you are considering Transformative Parenting™ as a spiritual path, the following story might be helpful:

I once had a patient who came to me because of disturbing visions and spiritual perceptions about people and places. She was a high-level practitioner, a senior member of her spiritual order. While having unusual perceptions was something she did not regard as odd for her, the character of the perceptions had changed recently to be more frightening, which caused her to seek me out for help.

As it turned out, she had for a long time been taking Ritalin to "improve her concentration", and was now at a high dose. Since I have seen stimulants cause psychosis in susceptible people, I recommended sharply reducing that medication. After doing that, and following some other suggestions, her symptoms subsided. All seemed well until I got an urgent call from her requesting an emergency supply of Ritalin. She was now on a retreat with her spiritual group, and found herself unable to do the meditation practices she had formerly been able to do quite comfortably.

I retell this story to make the point that it is very difficult to gauge one's actual spiritual progress in the presence of ongoing drug use. Some drugs can provide short-term experiences that are similar to high spiritual states. This can be useful, but it is a different thing from having the ability to attain a similar state without them.

Holding

Physical contact is an extremely important component of healthy psychological development. The simple observation of a baby crying in a bed or carrier, then quieting when picked up and held, is proof. When your child reaches towards you to be picked up, respond by doing so, and holding them. This is not difficult or expensive, but it is amazing how many parents have been conditioned to not hold their child, or to "wean them" from being held as quickly as possible out of fear their child is "manipulating them". Your child is not manipulating you, they have become afraid, and need reassurance that you are there to protect and love them.

While you are holding your child, be careful with "bouncing" them. Shaking can lead to concussion and brain damage, but is also used by ignorant or abusive parents to quiet children. Do not do it. Some parents are "bouncers" when soothing their children and others are "swayers". Gentle swaying, especially in your arms, is safest. If you tend to "bounce", be alert to any cues your child is finding it uncomfortable. Try swaying instead, it is safer; and whichever you do, be gentle.

From my experience, it is clear that holding your child deepens the empathic connection, which helps your ability to learn from each other. Do it as much as you can. Do your best to see from your child's view. Observe and acknowledge their need for loving physical contact, and re-learn from them the joy of holding and being held.

This leads to the issue of carriers, by which I mean strap-on-the-body carriers. Your child will be happiest and most secure, and you will be able to make constant adjustments for their comfort, if you hold them in your arms. I understand that not everyone has the strength for that, and so the next best thing can be using a carrier. My recommendation is to use a carrier where your child is strapped to your belly, sitting up, facing you, and has good head support if you are not holding their head constantly.

When I worked in Early Intervention, and later during my training in pediatrics, I was taught that many autistic children seemed to be more comfortable being carried facing away from their parent. While that may be the case for some children, removing the ability of you and your normal child to communicate visually also removes any chance of empathic attunement, or providing them with an experience of security or empowerment, much less omnipotence.

Use at least one hand at all times to touch or support your child's head while you walk. Babies can damage their necks easily, as their muscles have not developed well enough to support their swaying heads. Even when they are a bit older, but not able to walk well, they feel more secure if their heads are touched or supported.

Carrying children on your back, papoose style, is not recommend because empathic connection is lost, and you cannot determine if they are distressed. Similarly, when using a carriage or stroller, use one where you and your child can see each other, until they are older and more self-secure.

As your child gets a bit older, they may want to get out of the carrier or carriage, or they may want to ride without the straps attached. If we want our child to feel empowered this must be allowed if possible. Of course, this does not make your job any easier, but if it can be done with reasonable safety, it should be. The critical factor will be your ability to maintain constant awareness of your child.

Car safety seats can cause problems. If your child is struggling or in distress, I recommend safely stopping the car and letting them free for a while. Move on when they are calm, and/or you have found the source of their discomfort.

Co-Sleeping

Cultural issues notwithstanding, it is clear to my observation that little children prefer to sleep with their parents because of the security and comfort it provides. I am unsure why the current norm of separating children from parents at birth arose (perhaps concerns for abuse?), but there do exist many cultures where it is considered normal for children to sleep with their parents. My own bias, assuming a child will be safe from abuse, is to follow natural instinct as displayed by other primates, indeed most mammals, and to allow a child to sleep with or near their parents as they wish.

Besides the feeling of security for both you and your child, there are possible safety benefits. I remember clearly our own child twice having episodes of being unable to breathe during the night, and I am very grateful she was there, so I could turn her upside down and tap her back to clear her airway. I do not know that she would have died from Sudden Infant Death Syndrome if she had been in another room, but my impression was she might have.

On the other hand, if either parent has issues with drugs such as alcohol, or takes powerful sleeping medications (either of which might lead to inadvertent suffocation of the infant if the parent "passes out" and rolls over), it will be best to have their child sleep in the relative safety of their own crib or bed. The same is true if either parent has certain types of sleep disorders, or impulse-control issues.

At some point, different for each child, children will start wanting to sleep in their own bed. Although the transition may not be smooth or clean cut, here again, simply let your child be the guide.

Positioning Your Infant

In my opinion, infants should be rotated into various comfortable positions every few hours, or whenever it seems they are uncomfortable in their present position.

I disagree with the current thinking that children should be kept on their backs at all times when lying down; especially if there is a parent present and actively monitoring them. The mainstream belief is that lying on the back prevents inadvertent choking, but I have seen my daughter stop breathing when she was lying on her back, and I intervened to clear her airway.

Many times, I have observed clear signs of discomfort in infants that resolved with a shift in position. If you want your child to feel secure, a good first step is to assure they feel comfortable.

Physical therapists have told me that having infants on their bellies at least some of the time accelerates their ability to roll over and crawl. It also prevents the deformity in the back of the skull that can occur if a child is kept on their back.

As with all these recommendations, talk them over with your pediatrician or family doctor. It may be that your child requires specific handling, which I am not able to address here.

Dressing Your Child

For some reason, many parents over-bundle their children. It is true that swaddling a very young infant will calm it, but holding is the preferred way of calming a child. Swaddling a child can keep it warm, but again, holding is better.

In general, dress your child exactly as you yourself are dressed, until your child is able to convey their preference. Our pediatrician told us that you could perhaps add one thin layer, like a t-shirt, if you feel it necessary, especially for a newborn. Too many parents over-dress their child with heavy clothing or multiple layers, when the parents are dressed much more lightly. Their children often seem to be in obvious discomfort, seemingly unnoticed by their parents.

I once had a patient who told me that when her son was young, she would dress him extra warmly to make him easier to manage, since when he was hot, he was uncomfortable being active. In addition to totally ignoring her child's needs and wants, stifling their curiosity and physical development, and shutting down the parent-child empathic connection, this could have been dangerous, because of the risk of hyperthermia, and permanent damage to her child's brain.

At night, it is helpful to have your child near you so you can make quick adjustments to their covering. If your child is sweating, they are overdressed. If they are kicking off their blanket, or struggling to get out of their wrap or the sling, they may very well be too hot. Let your child tell you by their actions how much clothing or covering they need. If they are lethargic, or flush in the face, overheating might be the cause. Sometimes there is a particular place on the cheek or face that becomes red first, and you can use that as an early warning signal.

If your child feels cool to the touch, try covering them to make sure they are not cold, but if they keep kicking or pushing off their covers, you don't need to insist.

Infants and toddlers sometimes get cold and clammy in their body, yet are simultaneously very hot and sweaty around their heads. I interpret this as indicating a lot of metabolic activity is going on in their brains, and the sweating indicates a need to cool the brain while that activity is occurring. If you make them too warm, that brain activity will be curtailed, possibly to the detriment of their neurological development.

In summary, let your child show you what amount of clothing they need to be comfortable, whether it is more or less than you expect.

Breast-Feeding

Besides the well-known health benefits of breast-feeding, it is also a powerful reinforcer of the mother-child bond, and enhances empathic communication. I do not believe in any specific cut-off time for breast-feeding, as all the rules seem to be culturally based. A gradual weaning once a child is eating solid food seems reasonable, but it also seems fine to breast-feed even after they are eating solids as long as it isn't uncomfortable for the mother.

Pacifiers

A pacifier often helps, along with holding, to soothe a child. Suckling is a natural instinct, and has a clear calming and soothing effect. As in the case of breast-feeding, I do not see any reason to cut off a child from the pacifier at any particular age. The rules about this again seem mostly culturally based.

Some authorities claim pacifiers cause dental problems, but my review of the literature leads me to believe this concern is overblown. Forcing a child to suck their thumb or fingers is much more likely to lead to malocclusion than using a well-designed pacifier would. And denying a child the ability to orally self-soothe forces them to remain in distress, which runs counter to our aim of providing a feeling of security, much less a feeling of empowerment, or the illusion of omnipotence when possible.

Language Development

Much of the difficulty in providing an experience of security, empowerment, or omnipotence for your very young child is being able to know what their wants and needs are. Language is not just verbal, and as we discussed earlier, your child communicates with you even as a newborn if you are able to interpret his or her signals.

When they cry, you know something is uncomfortable for them, but a more subtle cue is turning their eyes away from whatever they had been looking at. Babies are overwhelmed easily, and if you can respect when that happens and stop doing whatever you are doing for a little while, you have just given them the experience of control over their environment - what I have been calling omnipotence. Conversely, when you see they are looking at something in the environment, consider they may be curious about it and either bring them towards the object or bring it to them to observe, touch, hold, and if safe, put in their mouths.

Another subtle example is when your child wants a pacifier, or to be fed. If you place the nipple to their lips and they root for it, they want it. If they look away, or move their head away, they do not. Don't make the mistake of automatically stuffing a pacifier or bottle into a baby's mouth to stop them from crying. Let them show you if it is what they want first. Perhaps they just want to be held.

Over time, you will become aware of other movements and sounds your child makes that indicate particular things they want, like their bottle, pacifier, or a favorite toy. Children create their own words and visual signs for things before they are able to repeat yours. Given the importance of optimal parent-child communication, learn and use your child's signs and words until they naturally transition to the use of adult language.

I once watched a father rapidly pushing his child down the sidewalk in a stroller. His child was making some insistent demand, which the father was either unable or unwilling to decipher. The father several times loudly shouted: "I can't understand what you're saying.", as his child sobbed, in between repetitions of his request. Consider the messages this father was inadvertently sending his child: "I don't understand you.", and "I don't care."

Learn from his mistake: If you do not understand what your child is trying to tell you, pause, hold them, and try to figure it out. If, after honestly trying for a while you still cannot understand them, apologize, and sit with their pain for a while before moving on. Then, at least they will know you tried.

Sign Language

Starting from a few months of age, I highly recommend learning some basic sign language, and using the signs simultaneously with audible words when interacting with your pre-verbal child. The ability to vocalize with formed words develops much later than the ability to communicate with hand gestures. (One of my daughter's first words was the sign for "more".) It is extremely empowering, for both you and your child, to be able to communicate wants and needs as early in life as possible. Sign language classes tailored for pre-verbal children and parents are available in many locations, as well as online. Using sign language will really give your child a head start in language development, and learning some basic signs is not hard. If it turns out your child is late developing verbal skills, it will not be such a big deal, because you will be able to communicate anyway. However, remember to have your child's hearing tested if they are late in developing speech.

Keep the Volume Down

Speaking of hearing, over the years our hearing becomes impaired, and the natural response is to turn up the volume; on our stereo, radio, TV, or our own voice. Children's hearing is much more sensitive, and they likely need (and would prefer) a lot less volume than you do. Be considerate of the fact that sound levels that might be comfortable for you could be painful and damaging for your child. Let them keep that good hearing as long as possible, by minimizing the volume of sound around them. If you have to be in a loud environment, allow them some type of hearing protection.

Autism

Autism spectrum disorder (ASD) is characterized by persistent deficits in social communication and social interaction. Though poorly understood, it seems reasonable to believe that symptoms result from a combination of genetic predisposition, and environmental factors.

One environmental benefit we can provide is a rich experience of social communication and interaction from the beginning. Transformative Parenting™, which emphasizes constant empathic communication and positive interaction between parent and child, should be helpful in mitigating the development of diagnosable ASD, or minimizing symptoms where the genetic predisposition is overwhelming.

Note that treatments used with already diagnosed autistic children commonly seek to maximize the development of communication skills in both parents and children, and utilize positive reinforcement (as opposed to negative reinforcement or punishment). These are natural outcomes of the Transformative Parenting™ process.

Attention Deficit Hyperactivity Disorder (ADHD)

ADHD is defined by levels of inattention, disorganization, and or hyperactivity and impulsivity which impair function and are abnormal for a child's age. As with ASD, I believe ADHD is likely due to the combined influence of genetic predisposition, and aggravating environmental factors, and that we as a society may be to blame for the explosive growth in these diagnoses. Here are several, potentially reversible factors, which I believe can exacerbate or cause these disorders:

The decline in stay-at-home parents, and the resulting placement of larger numbers of young children in potentially depersonalized group environments, leads to a lack of individual interaction with children, and less sensitivity to each child's unique needs for periods of calm, modulated stimulation, and exercise.

The elimination of physical education and recess (exercise through play) in schools, due to misguided cost cutting and the lack of understanding that even young children need to have outlets for nervous energy through physical activity, is a disaster. No wonder so many children are unmanageable. They have no way to manage their stress and energy, other than by "acting out" or taking medication.

When I worked in Early Intervention, I once met with a mother and her child who had been diagnosed with ADHD with hyperactivity. The mother told me that if she took her little girl to the playground for two hours a day, she was fine, and did not need medication. Unfortunately, she was unwilling to take her to the playground daily, and so her child needed to take stimulant medication almost every day so she could be "manageable" at home or at her daycare.

Another issue is excessive exposure to television, with its programmed 6-8 second frame shifts, and often violent and anxiety provoking content. A child's developing mind will adapt to the frequent frame shifts, and become accustomed to shifting attention every few seconds. As a result, when attention needs to be held for longer periods, say to solve a problem or create something, they find it difficult.

There is also a general, society-wide loss of parental attention. Parents are now preoccupied with being on the internet, texting, etc., instead of attending to their child. Children naturally want the attention of their parents, but all too often find their parents prefer to interact with a small or large box (phone, computer, or television), or talk to empty space (via Bluetooth headphones). Modeling their parents, children learn a restless, superficial way of attending to their environment, at least when not watching a television show or playing a video game.

Finally, some level of blame can be directed at psychiatrists, who sometimes use powerful stimulant medications to dampen children's "excessive" movement and inattention, instead of exploring and encouraging changes in parental behavior and environment to address the problem of hard-to-control children.

All of these issues can be minimized by choosing to practice Transformative Parenting™, learning and providing for your child's individual needs, and placing them above those of society's "norms".

Parental Conflict

Many people, despite my carefully reasoned arguments, may not agree with one or more core aspects of Transformative Parenting™; for example, the importance of providing your child a sustained experience of empowerment. One of those people may be your spouse.

The power of accumulated conditioning, peer pressure, and fear of the unknown (refer to the discussion of rigidity in the first chapter) are powerful forces which constrain all change. Understand first, that your spouse honestly feels their way is best, and may feel it is a dangerous mistake to help your child find their own way.

Though you must do your best to protect your child from outright physical or emotional abuse, you may be forced into compromise to ensure your marriage or partnership continues. This will necessarily trigger anxiety and emotional pain: for you, as your beliefs about what is best for your child come in conflict with those of your spouse, and for your child, who has their wants and needs overridden by their parents.

It is OK for parents to disagree, even in front of their children, as long they can do so calmly and respectfully. As we have learned, differences of opinion are inevitable, and trying to force the appearance of unity means one or the other parent must pretend to agree with the other. This is at best disempowering, and gives rise to tensions in the relationship, which are observed by their child.

Watching respectful disagreement and compromise is much better for a child than witnessing the subjugation of one parent by the other.

Children, like all of us, benefit from observing diverse ways of dealing with situations. From these observations, they (and hopefully parents) learn there are many ways to accomplish a given task.

It is most helpful if each parent can honor and respect that both the other parent and their child have valid points of view from their perspective. This opens space for compromise, and often finding common ground, which is a wonderful process for children to observe and copy.

Having said all that, it will save a prospective couple a lot of painful conflict if they discuss childrearing in some depth before making a long-term commitment to each other. I highly recommend discussing the ideas of Transformative Parenting™ ahead of time, while still in the "interviewing" phase of courtship.

Finally, as previously stated, Transformative Parenting™ is a best efforts endeavor. If you are doing the best you can, given your circumstances, you are doing well.

The "Willful" Child

A "willful" child is one who acts according to their own mind, and not necessarily according to the will of an adult or even their parent. Although a willful child is more difficult to manage for a parent because of their independence, the Transformative Parent™ accepts the task.

The Transformative Parent™ understands that they are purposefully raising their child in much the same way as a prince or princess, who will someday become a king or queen. We raise them to believe they are not to be dominated by anyone, at least internally. Necessarily, this will produce some level of rebelliousness towards their parents or other caregivers at times, especially when they do not understand why their desires can't or shouldn't be met.

This is the key to solving the problem. As an exercise in awareness, explain to your child what is going on, and why they must do what you ask, or why you cannot do what they ask. This reflection may well cause you to reconsider, or enable you to find a compromise. Sometimes though, there are no easy solutions, only difficult tasks. If that is the case, share their pain, and do what you must as gently as possible.

You will observe there is a difference between the independence of a child raised with a high degree of empowerment, and the rebelliousness of a child raised in a highly restrictive environment. The latter has learned that only by acting out (doing what they want to despite punishment or threats) can he or she have some semblance of autonomy or self-determination. The behavior of this child will be much more difficult to manage, as they have learned from experience that their parents and other adults cannot be trusted to take their point of view into consideration. Therefore, they mistrust and disregard even well-meaning guidance.

Violence

Aggression and violence are inherent parts of our nature as humans. We do violence to other creatures: we eat, kill, cage, torture, and displace them. We do violence to the environment: we exploit and pollute the air, land, and sea. We do violence to each other by killing, wounding, and exploiting each other in various ways. We must accept this before we can consider realistic ways of moderating the influence of these urges on our behavior.

Hitting and biting are behaviors that all children engage in at some point. Often, there is a clear purpose, but at other times, the reason is obscure.

Sometimes, when a child strikes a parent, it is a simple exploration of power. We can take instruction from observing a lioness with her cubs. Often, the cubs will "attack" their mother, playfully learning how to leap and bite. In the encounters I have witnessed, the mother and father cats are tolerant of their cubs' play. I encourage human parents to act the same way. Humans strike and kick to protect themselves, and it is natural that these behaviors arise in the play of children. On the other hand, children need exposure to empathy and concern for the feelings of others. If violent play leads to playmates being hurt, either physically or emotionally, it should be curtailed (non-violently), and the reason why explained.

Other times, children act out because they are being forced to do something they don't want to do. This is an extension of the pushing away that infants do when they need a break from a task. In this situation, where a traditional parent might become angry or administer punishment, the Transformative Parent™ will pause and reflect. It may be your child is being pushed to do something they do not want to, and they feel otherwise powerless to prevent it. In this case, striking you is part of a last ditch effort to communicate their point of view, and maintain some sense of empowerment.

The traditional parent, in administering punishment, believes they are teaching their child not to use violence to get what they want. In reality, they are teaching by example, the exact opposite. Punishment is violence, whether it involves striking, yelling, or otherwise causing pain to your child. By using punishment, you are demonstrating the use of violence by the powerful, against the powerless, to obtain what they want.

The Transformative Parent™, understanding this, will try to avoid using violence to counter their child's violent behavior.

The first priority is to remain calm. The second is to try to understand why your child is upset, and regain your empathic connection. Is he or she tired, hungry, sad, engaged in something important to them that you have inadvertently overlooked? Are they safe? Do they need your attention, love, holding? Do they need space? Is what you want them to do more important than addressing these primary needs? If not, take care of your child's need first. If what you need done is a priority, it is important that you take the time to help your child understand why. If you are not sure why what you want is a priority, perhaps it is not, and the demand should be retracted. "Because I say so" is a poor rationale, and does nothing to further self-awareness in the parent, or trust and security in their child.

Develop a willingness to compromise with your child. Can you offer a choice: A different shirt, or a different color? Can they watch the end of their show and then brush their teeth? Do they want to use the green toothbrush or the red one? Giving options gives back some power to your child, and helps them see you as their ally. Often it is helpful to step back and look at the larger picture. Is there another way to accomplish the overall goal that is more in line with your child's needs and wants? Offer the option, and if your child comes up with their own option, so much the better.

The use of violence by one child against another to get what they want must be handled carefully. One suggestion is to separate the combatants, and allow both a cooling off period. If there are disputes over property, they should be mediated by parents who hopefully can model a calm sense of fairness and justice. If, after the short separation there is a resumption of violence, separate the children for a longer period. This way, the frustration can be explored and hopefully mitigated and whoever is instigating the violence will learn that violence leads to an interruption in play. The other child will also feel secure and protected.

Again, there is a difference between the experimentation with violence that occurs with children raised with a high level of personal authority (as in Transformative Parenting™), and the violent behaviors shown by children who have been raised in a highly restrictive or violent environment. The latter will be much more difficult to manage, and there may be no recourse but to exclude such a playmate (and their parents) from interaction with less violent children, especially if intervention with the parents is unsuccessful.

Spare the Rod

I've made this point before, but it is extremely important, and so I'm going to repeat it. Punishment poisons a child-parent relationship. It ruins the trust a child should have that their parent understands them and is looking after their best interest, and/or it creates a belief within a child (their self-object model) that they are broken, inadequate, or "bad".

If it is necessary to inject disappointment into a child's world model, it should be in the form of a *natural consequence* as much as possible.

One winter, I was outside walking when I met a woman at a street corner with her two children. The older one, a girl about eight years old, wasn't wearing a coat and was obviously cold. I asked the mother about it, and she told me her daughter had stubbornly refused to wear a coat today: "She insisted she didn't need it." Although the mother might have brought the coat anyway, this is a good example of a natural consequence.

The daughter made a mistake, but learned a lesson about winter, and her resistance to cold as a result. Likely she will be more cautious about leaving her coat at home in the future. She also knows that her mother tried to protect her, but nonetheless was willing to grant her autonomy. Likely she will also be more receptive to her mother's recommendations in the future.

Punishment is usually a result of anger. If you have control over your anger, you will have much less of an impulse to punish.

Understand that your child either made a mistake, or did what they honestly felt was most appropriate under the circumstances. The same as we all do. Either way, anger is inappropriate. If it was a mistake, it keeps you from understanding that it was a mistake. If it was not a mistake, it keeps you from being able to understand their point of view.

Generally, if your child has offended you, or is resisting you, you should evaluate the situation and determine the cause. What change can you make, that will enable a solution you can both agree with, without resorting to punishment?

For example, parents who maintain a highly stimulating environment (such as TV, or loud music) right up until bedtime are going to find it frustrating getting their children to sleep. A solution would be to have a "winding down" routine, providing a calm environment, and an established pattern to going to bed. Though perhaps asking a lot, if the parents go to bed around the same time, children will not worry about "missing anything".

Fundamentalist Christians sometimes use Proverbs 13:24 and 23:13 to justify punishment of children. For them, I invoke Jesus' words in Matthew 18, note Jesus' gentle character, his admonishment to "turn the other cheek", and point out that according to Christian belief the words and actions of Jesus supersede the Old Testament. Also note that the words ".. spare the rod and spoil the child" actually come from an erotic poem written by Samuel Butler. He was abused by his father as a child, and was known to have a very poor regard for his parents in later life.

Circumstances in my childhood sometimes required me to go on long bus trips unaccompanied by adults, either alone or with my younger siblings. On one such trip, I remember meeting an elderly woman, who fascinated me with descriptions of her childhood, a world without electricity or automobiles. She also shared her bitterness that her children now had little to do with her. In a flash of childhood insight, I asked if she had shown them love growing up. She answered, "I taught them respect".

I have a very dear acquaintance who was beaten by his mother every day, after she got home from work. Not because he did anything wrong, but because that is what the other mothers in the neighborhood did. The predictable outcome was that he had a very strained relationship with her in later life.

From these stories, we learn that the respect born from fear is temporary.

I have been told you should beat your child at least once when they are four or five, so they will fear you when they are older and do what you say. Don't do it. The submission and "respect" you gain will be temporary, and a poor substitute for the long lasting respect, honor, and esteem you will obtain by showing love.

Teach your children love, by giving and demonstrating love, and they will love you always. Teach them "respect" through punishment, and you will probably not get love, and likely not respect, once they are old enough not to fear you.

> *"Always be nice to your children because they are the ones who will choose your rest home."*
> *- Phyllis Diller*

Conclusion

We are approaching the end of our journey. Thank you for your efforts, I know it has been a struggle in some places.

We are now more aware of the pervasiveness of our unconscious mental conditioning. We discovered we are all products of this conditioning, which has occurred throughout the course of our lifetimes. Because of that conditioning, and the process of objectification, we have all created unique mental models, which we use to understand all of the objects in our universe, both external and internal, including traits and characteristics we believe to be true about ourselves. We have explored some of the positives and negatives inherent in this process.

We have learned that our conditioning has been less than optimal, and has resulted in the creation and maintenance of faulty object models about ourselves and others that limit us, cause us unnecessary pain and suffering, and lead us to cause unnecessary pain and suffering in others.

Although learning is necessary for any higher-level organism to survive in a complex world, because of how we learn, and a lack of awareness of the limitations of that process, we feel anxiety, and are in conflict with others and ourselves.

We learned about the state of enlightenment, which by pausing the process of objectification, allows us an opportunity to undo the effects of our conditioning and free us from unnecessary suffering. We also learned that paths to reach the state of enlightenment have largely been unavailable to average people, living ordinary lives, and without access to enlightened teachers to guide them.

It has been my honor to share with you a path towards ever-increasing awareness, sensitivity, and control, which is available to all parents. To any parent who is willing to allow their child to teach them, and is willing to put forth the effort to undo their faulty conditioning.

By following the methods of Transformative Parenting™, you will discover and undo faulty conditioning in yourself, and build a base of positive, self-image enhancing conditioning in your child. This, and your ongoing awareness, will provide some needed protection from the often faulty and negative social messaging, which is pervasive in modern life.

While training to be a psychiatrist, one of my peers shared with me his desire to discover a vaccination that would help protect against mental illness. I believe I have discovered it: the establishment of a secure, empathic, empowering relationship with a parent in early childhood, through the practice of Transformative Parenting™.

In all cultures, there are forces that demand submission and conformance to the norm. Although these norms are based on imperfect models of reality, conforming may be required. For example, in some cultures women are taught to be submissive to men and that they are worth less than men are. The same message is heard by slaves with respect to their owners, or to Jews with respect to Nazi's, or to Palestinians with respect to Jews, or to Muslims with respect to Christians or vice versa. Depending on each person's culture and circumstance, each of these beliefs has a certain amount of relative validity or credibility.

We have come to recognize that these beliefs, and many others we have, are relative realities - products solely of cultural conditioning. Although we may not be in a position to act on that recognition, given the culture or circumstance we find ourselves in, internally we can be aware and thus somewhat free of their limiting effect. We will also be more flexible and adaptive when our circumstances change.

If our world is to survive, for the sake of our children and their children, we are going to have to make great changes as a species. Our genetically imposed and culturally reinforced programming causes us to be competitive and exploitative. As a species we cannot rest, we must always be conquering, dominating and acquiring. This has gotten us to where we are - the dominant species on the planet, inventors and exploiters extraordinaire. However, like a cancer which cannot be stopped, we will be the cause our own demise unless we learn to restrain ourselves.

> *"We must learn to live together as brothers or perish together as fools."*
>
> *- Martin Luther King, Jr.*

By becoming aware of your conditioning, and by "vaccinating" as it were, your children from unconscious cultural conditioning, we will be able to chart a new path.

There are problems to conquer that do not require the subjugation of other people, other life forms, or the pollution of our planet. If we learn to temper our competitive and aggressive urges, we can work together to create a sustainable way of being, while respecting the other life forms which support us in the matrix of life. We can learn to become better stewards of the planet and the gifts we have been given.

It is time for humanity to mature as a species. I trust we are not too late.

Altruism is not highly regarded in our culture; mostly we are conditioned to its opposite: self-interest. If this is true for you, I have this advice: Do not practice Transformative Parenting™ for humanity, do it for yourself. Note that because of our conditioning few of us ever attain happiness for more than brief periods - because happiness has been defined for us as conquering. We "get" something we desire, and it makes us briefly happy. Then the happiness goes away, and we must dominate, conquer, or acquire something else. With awareness, we can modify this conditioning. We can be happier with what we have, find pleasure in self-discovery, and joy in helping others less fortunate. This is an amazing gift to give yourself, and to pass on as an inheritance to your child.

> *"The secret of happiness, you see, is not found in seeking more, but in developing the capacity to enjoy [having] less."*
> *- Socrates*

There is a joy in living, which is inherent. Life is a great gift we have been given. Moreover, to be born human, a member of the dominant species, well that is even more special.

Most of us have been taught it is wrong to feel joy and gratitude in simply being, and because of this teaching, we lose that joy. I have seen it though, in the faces of people doing the most menial tasks, in holy men dressed in rags, poor mothers feeding their children, and husbands proudly introducing me to their families crowded into tiny ramshackle apartments. Most of all, I see it in the faces of small children who are treated well by their parents.

I once observed a crippled young man in Delhi, cleaning a shirt in the river Ganges. He was one of many menial workers who were cleaning the clothes of the well-to-do by alternately soaking them in the river, then swinging them up in great circular arcs and down onto large boulders.

As he pounded the stains from the fabric of the shirt he was working on, without the benefit of detergent or soap; bare chested, wearing only a wrap of cloth around his waist, I watched him at his steady work. His large, well-muscled upper body was a stark contrast to his tiny shriveled legs.

After a while, he turned aside from his task briefly, and noticed me watching. His face opened into a broad smile, and his chest swelled. I felt the pride that filled him as he turned back to his work, showing me how well he was doing his job, which could only have paid pennies a day, but was perhaps enough for him to be meagerly self-sufficient.

I learned quite a lot from this young Master, though we never spoke, and I watched him only once for a little while.

You have the opportunity to learn even more profound lessons from your child. All it takes is eyes that are willing to look, ears that are willing to listen, and a heart that is willing to feel.

I wish you and your child every happiness, and lives filled with wondrous experience.

"And a woman who held a babe against her bosom said,
Speak to us of Children.
And he said:
Your children are not your children
They are the sons and daughters of Life's longing for itself.
They come through you but not from you,
And though they are with you yet they belong not to you.
You may give them your love, but not your thoughts,
For they have their own thoughts.
You may house their bodies but not their souls,
For their souls dwell in the house of tomorrow,
which you cannot visit, not even in your dreams.
You may strive to be like them, but seek not to make them like you.
For life goes not backward nor tarries with yesterday.
You are the bows
from which your children as living arrows are sent forth.
The archer sees the mark upon the path of the infinite, and He
bends you with His might that His arrows may go swift and far.
Let your bending in the archer's hand be for gladness;
For even as He loves the arrow that flies,
so He loves also the bow that is stable."
- Khalil Gibran

Epilogue

"A good book has no ending." – Robert Frost

Being present with your child is the most important thing, but if you have some free time, visit our website:

www.TransformativeParenting.org.

There, you can share your thoughts, ask questions, find up-to-date information about our advocacy and outreach efforts, and explore ways you can help spread the ideas of Transformative Parenting™.

If you know people who might benefit from hearing about Transformative Parenting™, please share with them your understanding, a copy of this book, or a link to the website.

CPSIA information can be obtained at www.ICGtesting.com
Printed in the USA
BVOW11s1439180915

418373BV00002B/2/P